NEA:
PROPAGANDA FRONT
OF
THE RADICAL LEFT

BY

Sally D. Reed

NEA: Propaganda Front of the Radical Left

Art work by Dick Hafer

DEDICATION

To my family and friends who have shown their unwavering support throughout the years and to those who share the NCBE vision, especially Mrs. Dale Evans/Rogers, Dr. Paul Busiek, Steve and Terry.

Table of Contents

Introduction
by Dale Evans-Rogers.

In the late forties, my husband and I began to notice a decline in patriotism, along with a shift toward "One-World-Ism" in our public school teaching. We realized that a definite attempt by some of our educators was being made to discredit, in a subtle way, this country in the minds of our children.

In every personal appearance program, in addition to television programs, we made a practice of leaving our audience with a "God and Country" salute. We encountered much criticism, even to the point of losing a television variety show.

Well do I remember the son of a friend who attended a progressive school in the forties. This boy was allowed to do his thing, whatever he felt like doing, instead of being required to learn his letters, numbers - and discipline.

The Bible states that the fear of the Lord is the beginning of wisdom. Those who would destroy the values that made this country strong and great, have been quietly manuevering for years to bring about an overthrow of our freedom under God, our Judeo-Christian heritage. Take a look at the fruits of their labors among our young: Crime, dope addiction, alcoholism, prostitution, free-wheeling sex and abortion - and saddest of all, suicide, which is growing at an enormous rate.

Now, you may or may not agree, nor understand everything in this book, but I implore you to read it and investigate the claims as stated.

One of our children came home from Junior High School and asked, "Mom, what do you know about Benedict Arnold"? I replied: "I was taught that he was a traitor to this country." Then our daughter stated; "Our social studies teacher said he didn't blame Benedict Arnold for what he did, that our government promised him a sum of money to spy on the British and then refused to pay him, that he had a sick wife and hungry children". Then she added: He asked us if we didn't agree with Benedict Arnold. To say I was shocked is an understatement. The problem was that I was too busy filming our television series instead of stating my complaint at the PTA or the School Board.

Don't these underground gophers of subversion realize that this country is free because the very values we have fought for come from the standard of Almighty God in His book, the Bible?

I care about the children coming after me. God have mercy on those who would destroy their freedoms and ultimately, the freedoms of those who are attempting to destroy the underpinnings of a free America.

Please read this book slowly and comprehensively, and do what you can, where you are, to speak, vote and pray for sanity in our public schools.

Respectfully,

Dale Evans Rogers

CHAPTER

1

Imagine the educational bureaucracy in Washington being controlled by persons with views and politics directly opposed to your own—in the areas of parenting, family decisions, and religious beliefs.

Imagine people who prefer power for themselves to education for your children, and want to pull the strings of education in your local community from centralized offices in Washington D.C.

Imagine people who oppose the free enterprise system in America, openly advocate socialism, and call for the disarmament of this country so that the Soviet Union would defeat it and establish a World Order.

Imagine these things, and you will not be far from the truth. These people exist, and they are in control of public education in America.

An organization called the National Education Association (NEA) has wrung control of the public schools from parents and local communities and placed it in its own offices. In 1976 this teachers' union got a political payoff for supporting President Carter—the Department of Education (DOE).

Together the NEA and the DOE have been waging a campaign of terror against public education and parents' rights to control the lives of their children.

It is a nightmare. Not too long ago American education

3

was controlled democratically by parents and school boards elected by parents.

Local communities were able to teach their children ideas and values that they chose to teach them. Religion was not kicked out of the public schools. Taxpayers and parents made their own decisions about whether they wanted programs like busing and affirmative action in their schools—in most cases they decided not.

But parents have unwittingly relinquished control of education to the NEA. This militant union does not consider local schools to be an extension of the home and the parent. Rather, it considers the school a means to steer children *away* from parents ideas and values.

If parents had had a choice in deciding whether they wanted to introduce the "new math" in schools, would they ever have said yes? Of course not. Parents know that two and two make four. Parents know that the "new math" won't help anyone balance a checkbook.

Shouldn't parents have the right to *choose* whether they want biblical creation or evolution taught in the schools? Or should this decision be made in the courts and by the NEA union?

As of now—the NEA and the courts have already settled those questions: in their favor. Not only does the NEA not want parent's morality taught in schools: it wants immorality flaunted in the classrooms. Not only is religion expelled from the school, but atheism and secularism is promoted and praised.

The NEA is an advocate of "situation ethics." This philosophy teaches that nothing is right or wrong. Whatever you decide to do in a given situation is right for you.

One third grader came home from school in tears because his teacher told him to play a "game" in which the

4

US was under seige from the Soviet Union, having built up its nuclear weapons to the point of provoking a war.

The teacher asked the student to get under a desk, which was supposed to represent a cave in which the child was hiding from the Russians and nuclear radiation.

The problem? There was only enough food in the cave for two. And the child is in the cave with his mom and dad, so the child must decide which of them must leave the cave and die.

No wonder the child was filled with guilt and self-hate when he came home. This is, by the way, a true story. It illustrates the values and pressure that are being thrust on our children in the name of "modern, progressive education."

The way to save education from the radicals and the so-called reformers is to return it to the parents and the local communities, where it belongs. Schools should teach materials selected by parents, not by national unions trying to influence social change.

Today the NEA is stubborn about its influence. It insists upon its right to maintain a strangle-hold on American education. Parents' questions about vital educational issues are dismissed as the screams of bigoted reactionaries. If parents say they are opposed to busing they are branded as racists.

The saddest thing of all is that many parents have absolutely no idea that the NEA has seized all power to itself and has entirely cut communities out of educational decision-making.

One way the NEA does this is to encourage the consolidation of school districts. Many parents go along with this because they do not know what it means. The NEA promises that larger school districts mean more money, and more money means better facilities for students: better microscopes, better gymnasiums, more audio-visual equipment.

But parents must remember that while larger school districts may mean more of some things and better of others, these facilities are now spread over a much larger group of students, so that the value that each child derives from consolidation may actually be less.

More importantly, consolidation of school districts is a way for the NEA to wrest control of schools from parents and place it in the hands of bureaucrats, preferably bureaucrats controlled by the offices of the NEA. The smaller the school district the more malleable it is to the wishes of parents. The larger it gets, the less control parents have, the less attention your child gets.

The NEA is a classic example of how special interest politics can overwhelm the national interest. As this book will document, the NEA is essentially uninterested in what is good for children, or in what parents want for their children.

Instead the NEA is interested mainly in collecting fabulous amounts of money for itself which it uses for left-wing political campaigns, and also to propagate the idea that a New World Order is needed to solve the inequities of the free enterprise system.

John Boyles, editor of a Washington based bulletin, *Educator's Newsletter*, writes that "The day is fast approaching when the schools will be acknowledged for what they are becoming: society's agreed-upon vehicle for instituting social change.

"There appears to be no alternative to acknowledging that we have created a way of living in which public employees will perform a significant fraction of functions traditionally left to families."

Boyles went on to remark that "Marx and other theoreticians of social change—Lenin, Gandhi, and Mao Tse Tung—have all spoken of the necessity of destroying the traditional fabric of family life in order to accomodate the needs of society undergoing economic transformation."

If this educational trend continues, and if the NEA is allowed to get its way for much longer, we may well lose our national freedoms and become a totalitarian state. Because this is nothing less than what the NEA is advocating: the abolition of our freedoms.

In the area of education, the NEA has already stolen these freedoms from parents and taxpayers. It is now on its way to raising a new generation of radicals to achieve its goal of destroying America as the founding fathers envisioned it, as we and our forefathers have worked so hard to make it.

This is a call for parents to rise up and prevent Soviet-style control from being imposed on our children and on our lives. The only way this can be done is for parents to recapture their legitimate rights as secured in the Constitution and the Bill of Rights.

Let me begin by discussing two conflicting theories of education. One may be described as the theory of Specialized Control of education, and it is subscribed to by the NEA. The other is the theory of Parental Control of education, and it is accepted by the vast majority of the American people.

Think about this question: Who should control the education of your child? This large question is related to others: Why do you send your child to school? Is it to gain expert knowledge of a sort you do not possess? Or is it because you, who must work to support your family, need someone to act as a surrogate for you, imparting those ideas and values in your child that you otherwise would have done?

There are other ways to put the first question: Should teachers have the final say about what ideas and values are transferred to your children? Or should you? Perhaps neither: perhaps the school board or the administration of public schools should decide everything. But in that case should the school board represent anybody? Parents? The state?

Two schools of thought have emerged in answer to these questions. The school of Specialized Control believes that parents have little or no role in their children's education. That is because parents are old-fashioned, a bit undereducated, products of a different time, with silly moralistic ideas that they want to impose on their children.

This school feels that students, if condemned to learn from their parents, would hardly get an education; instead they would pick up all kinds of ignorant ideas and develop phobias. Students should be redeemed from their parents and placed in the hands of specialists, who understand what is needed for them to prosper and flourish in this modern, complex society of ours.

Now Americans have a great deal of trust in experts. After all "experts" are responsible for the great technological advances this country has made. Division of labor makes it impossible not to have "experts" in just about every field. Perhaps it is true, after all, that there are experts in the field of education who are better equipped than parents to raise the children.

I don't agree with this. You see, education is not a discipline in and of itself; rather, it is a graft on several disciplines. Education is not about itself; it is about history, math, English, science, and physics. More broadly interpreted, education is about knowledge, manners, and physical training.

I obviously realize that there can be experts in these specialized fields: experts in history and math and physical education. These experts are called teachers. And their legitimate function is not being denied.

Nobody questions that a history teacher should play an important role in what is being taught as history. Or that a physics teacher should explain the laws of Newton without visiting parents offering their own explanations.

But who decides in what broad framework all these courses should be taught? Which disciplines should be stressed and which underplayed? What values should be transmitted? Whether the school should be a vocational or a more liberal arts oriented school?

I believe that the parents should decide these questions of the direction of the schools which educate their kids. Why parents? For two reasons. First, it is their children who are being educated. Second, they pay for the schools.

Take point one. I believe that parents send their children to school to get the education that they cannot, for various reasons, provide themselves. Parents do not mean their children's education to be restricted to what they learned in school. Times change; we know that.

But while parents understand that there is new knowledge available, and children must be kept up with the times, they know also that there is much hokum being passed off as new and modern knowledge. Mainly values which parents overwhelmingly reject are being systematically drilled into children, and these values are self-gratification, hedonism, promiscuity, agnosticism or atheism, and a sympathy for violence when committed by the poor and minority groups.

All this is hailed by "progressive."

It is a fact today that many of our so-called experts are not experts at all. They simply pose as specialists. And they use their self-appointed titles to impose views on your children.

And they reject the notion that parents should be actively involved in their children's education because they do not want parents to know what they are teaching the children. Deep down, they know parents will be angry, and might even revolt.

Parents should control the atmosphere in which their children are educated because it is *their* children who are being educated; they have the greatest stakes in the matter. Teachers, who are transient officials, have no necessary interest in the welfare of the child.

This does not mean some teachers don't take an interest in the children they teach. Nor does it mean that you have to father or mother a child to be interested in its upbringing. But it is true nevertheless that many teachers today have been driven by the NEA to think more about salary and politics than about children's education. It was easier for the NEA to steer teachers to this position than it would have been to make parents think this way. That's because parents have, do, and always will care most about their children's education: it's their flesh and blood.

Point two, stated earlier, is that parents pay for public education through taxes. So their interest in it is also fiduciary. Teachers don't pay for education; they are paid by it. That makes parents the boss, and teachers the employees assigned to specific functions.

In any company it is the guy who pays the salary who makes legislative decisions. It is the guys who are paid who carry them out. So it should be in education. Parents should govern the ethos of the schools—not making narrow, specific decisions, but generating broad policy. And teachers and administrators should carry it out.

The NEA wants to get parents out of education. While sounding platitudes about helping facilitate parent-teacher relationships, getting parents involved, and so on, the NEA has nevertheless affirmed that final jurisdiction in education belongs to teachers, and because the NEA represents teachers, it belongs to the NEA. Parents should help out when they're needed, but they should butt out when they aren't wanted.

The Report of the Committee on Resolutions of the NEA stated clearly in 1934, "The National Education Association *unqualifiedly* endorses the principle that *all* school affairs, including budgets and the appointments of teachers and officials, should be under the management of school authorities without interference from political or other special groups."

Parents are dismissed as another "special group."

The argument for parents' rights is connected to another argument I want to make: for local control of education over federal control. Again, I am at odds with the NEA in this.

Why local control? Because it is more efficient. Schools can be more flexible if they are governed locally than if all the decisions are made in Washington, either in Congress or in the offices of the NEA.

Secondly, local schools are more accountable to those who pay for it, whose children occupy the seats in the classroom. In other words parents can more easily be involved in locally controlled education than in federally run education.

Third, local control allows for the presentation of different branches of knowledge. In Arizona certain subjects may be introduced which are relevant to the state; in Alaska these subjects may be irrelevant, but there the schools may want to teach about ice-fishing or the oil pipeline.

So also local control makes it possible for different areas to teach their own set of values to children. We don't want a federally mandated set of values being imposed on our children. But neither do we want no values being taught at all.

Local education means that in Salt Lake City, Utah the Mormons can teach values associated with their faith. I don't mean theology (I accept the principle of separation of church and state) but it is possible to teach morality without violating the First Amendment.

Parents in New York City might not want their children to receive the same values as the parents in Salt Lake City, even though the values themselves may be unimpeachable: honesty, decency, dignity, etc. The point is: parents in local areas would be able to choose for themselves what they want to impart to their children.

What does the NEA think about local control of education?

Said the 1941 Resolutions Committee of the NEA:

"The NEA urges that the federal government expropriate funds for public education.

"The NEA urges the reorganization of small school districts into larger ones.

"Lay boards should be guided by the recommendations of professional educators.

"School budgets should be prepared by the school superintendent and his staff and approved by the board of education."

And so on. The point is only thinly veiled: Professionals over parents. State control over local control.

And lest you think the NEA has abandoned its doctrine since 1941, not so.

The NEA's legislative agenda to the 98th Congress, calling for one-third federal funding for education, and for the national NEA to control educational decisions on behalf of teachers, make that clear.

The NEA has consistently supported the doctrine of "compelling interest" on the part of states and the federal government. This doctrine says that since states and the federal government have a direct interest in the welfare of the child, they are as qualified as the child's parent in controlling the child's education.

So now your son or daughter has three parents: the real ones, and Uncle Sam.

And the illegitimate parent, Uncle Sam, assumes the right to decide finally what is good for your child. In many cases the government does not merely act "in loco parentis," or instead of the parent, but it acts "contra parentis," against the wishes of the parent.

The NEA also declared its affection for federal control of education when it lobbied aggressively for the "Department of Education" during the 1976 election. This it got for its endorsement of candidate Jimmy Carter.

The Department of Education was a shameless giveaway by a politician with no sense of ethics. Jimmy Carter posed as a moralist but in fact he was an opportunist. He traded a cabinet department for a special interest endorsement, and as a result, in the words of one NEA official, "We became the first union with a cabinet post of our own."

Now more decisions about education could be made in Washington. Needless to say parents role in education would be further diminished. And bureaucrats in the capital, mostly influenced by bureaucrats at the NEA, would wield more and more power, and collect more and more money.

Recently the NEA released a document "Values and Valuing—Parents and Students" which made its case for modern (its own) values over traditional (parents') values.

"Schools are becoming increasingly involved in values education," the NEA brochure said. Then, anticipating that the values being taught would not be the ones parents would approve of, the NEA said, "It is natural that parents should react to this values education with mixed feelings."

Then begins the NEA attack on traditional values. "A few (parents) may even wonder if values education is valid if it leads young people to explore and analyze, rather than accept, the traditional values of our society."

Of traditional values the NEA opines, "When we consider our national values, we sometimes like-to think back to the 'good old days' at a time when our country was largely agricultural."

What a gross misrepresentation. Traditional values were taught in America as late as a couple of decades ago.

Yet the NEA makes it look like the Judeo-Christian ethic went out in the 18th century. What they fail to understand is right and wrong has nothing to do with time. Truth is an absolute and does not vary depending on whether society is agricultural based or urbanized.

"Young people grow up in a much more complex world," the NEA says, so it is necessary "to establish modes of alternative problem-solving for the future."

The new values education will consist of teaching students to deal with "the continuing possibility of holocaust as the result of the proliferation of nuclear weapons, the possibility of world hunger resulting from unplanned industrial growth, uncertain climatic conditions, over-population, the possibility of genetic engineering, and the changing definitions of life and death.''

Some of these are legitimate value-questions that it is necessary for students to probe. But notice who decides which values are modern, which questions must be discussed, and which values are outdated, which questions must be excluded.

Answer: the NEA.

One thing particularly insidious about NEA ''specialists'' deciding what your child shall learn and what ethics he or she shall live by is that if you disagree with what is being taught you don't have an alternative.

Many years ago it used to be that parents could simply pull their children out of school and teach them at home. But now uniform state certification of all teachers prohibits all but certified parents from teaching at home.

So if you don't like the public schools today, you have only one option: put your child in private school. That means you will be paying double for your kid's education. You will be paying state taxes which will pay for public education, even though you don't avail yourself of it. And you will be paying private school tuition.

The NEA's plan to control education consists of making all alternatives to NEA domination either illegal or extremely impractical.

Unlike the NEA, the National Commission on Excellence said that parents have an important role to play in education:

''You bear a responsibility to participate actively in your child's education. You should encourage more diligent study and discourage satisfaction with mediocrity and the attitude which says 'let it slide'; monitor your child's study;

encourage good study habits, encourage your child to take more demanding rather than less demanding courses; nurture your child's curiosity, creativity, and confidence; and be an *active participant* in the work of the schools." (Emphasis added.)

Now what does the NEA say about parents who want to exercise a role in their children's education?

First, it calls them fascists and hate-mongers. Says Terry Herndon, former executive director of the NEA and still a force in its management, "I say to you that a cohort of chronic tax resisters, congenital reactionaries, dangerous witch hunters, energized super-patriots, wayward dogma peddlers, and vitriolic race haters have coalesced into a sophisticated political force that has nearly overwhelmed a too comfortable and too stale progressive political movement."

In other words if you don't agree with the policies of the NEA, and want to exercise some say in your own son's education, you're a bigot and a crazy man.

The NEA held a Conference on the New Right last year. The New Right is the NEA's code word for parents. It chooses to attack parents not directly but by attacking the New Right. Thus it hopes to discredit the very notion of parents' rights in education by discrediting the conservative political movement which goes by the name of "New Right."

During the NEA New Right conference it attacked the notion that education should be decentralized and localized. This it equated with turning the public schools over to the Ku Klux Klan.

"We see this as an attack on opportunities for minorities and women . . . an attempt to implement the Bakke decision on affirmative action programs." So said John Ryor, former

NEA president. Only he knew what he was talking about. But the message was clear that evening: parents, go home.

At the New Right conference the NEA also issued attacks on those who opposed then President Carter's Comprehensive National Health Insurance and other spending programs. The NEA voted in favor of SALT II and deplored "another multi-billion dollar arms race." The NEA found even President Carter too right-wing, and came out deploring his efforts to reduce the budget slightly for austerity.

Again, anyone who opposed these political goals of the top echelons of the NEA were said to be racists and reactionaries.

A few months ago the NEA launched another attack on parents' rights in the name of a campaign to control "censorship."

Now "censorship" is a legal term which refers to banning books. I do not favor censorship. But censorship is not what is at issue in classrooms. Rather, the question is: who gets to choose which books are placed in curricula and libraries, who decides just what values and ideas are transmitted to our children?

Understood this way, censorship is simply a matter of opinion. Should the NEA decide what books your children read? Should the government decide? Or should parents and elected school boards decide? This question has nothing to do with an author's right to publish. It has everything to do with parents' right to control the education of their children.

For the NEA, when its bureaucrats decide the curriculum, that's "academic freedom." When parents decide, that's "censorship." Also the NEA has a very selective view of censorship. It regards any attempt to remove obscene or filthy texts from classrooms as censorship. But it remains silent as feminists rewrite the Bible to remove "sexist" references, or black power groups rewrite *Huckleberry Finn* to delete "racist" imagery.

The NEA is developing its own acceptable curriculum which includes courses inveighing against the arms race and the current Administration. But books favorable to the present defense policies are systematically (though quietly) —should we say the word?—censored. Yes, the NEA supports censorship—as long as they are the ones doing the censoring.

NEA Today, published by the teachers' union, recently published an article "Textbooks Under Fire" in which it alleged that laws permitting parents to have a say in texts "is a process for the conservative New Right . . . to influence the choice of books used in the nation's classrooms."

Of course it is: but it is also a process for *all* parents to exercise their rights. What's wrong with that? The NEA treats the very idea of a parent reading his child's textbook as gravely subversive of the Constitution.

NEA Today laments, "The Alabama Education Association fought unsuccessfully this year to keep its state legislature from increasing the proportion of lay citizens on the state textbook committee."

In other words, if you don't like what the parents say, kick them off the committee. Let the NEA have sole voice over children's education, not because they pay for the education, not because it's their children, but because they gain in money and power from this control.

The area of "Child Abuse" is an example of how central, or more precisely NEA, control of education can lead to absurd guidelines and rules.

Now obviously child abuse is a serious crime which should not be permitted. But here are some of the signs the

NEA *Journal of Education* asks teachers to look for in reporting child abuse:

—"If a parent is reluctant to share information about the child."

—"If a parent has unrealistic expectations for the child."

—"If a parent is very strict and a disciplinarian."

Now come on. Are these evidence of child abuse? It just shows the mentality that can develop when you sit on a national committee. It just shows what the "experts" can get mixed up in when common sense (which parents have) is kept locked out of the meeting.

Parents should not feel bashful to assert their legitimate rights with respect to their children's education. These rights were intended for them by the Founding Fathers and are embodied in our Constitution. Parents should also insist on alternatives to the monopoly system of public education, or at least the monopoly system of the NEA controlling all of public education. Public education should be run at the local level; then it enjoys advantages of efficiency and flexibility that private education does. Also public education should not be the only option available to parents. Private education competes with public education and makes public education better. Also private education gives parents whose views are in a minority an alternative to the public schools. If you live in New York City and they want to teach cannibalism to the kids there, you see, you can send your kid elsewhere.

2

We all know that Johny can't read, but do we also know that he can't write or think for himself? Do we know that Johny's teacher can barely read and write?

The educational situation in this country has gotten dramatically worse during the last few decades. This has occurred despite the facts that literally billions of dollars have been ploughed into education, and the most modern educational theories were put into effect. The result? As columnist Patrick Buchanan puts it, "Out came the dumbest young generation we have produced."

Precisely how rotten the state of American public education is was catalogued by the National Commission on Excellence in its 1983 report. The bipartisan commission warned that "The educational foundations of our society are being eroded by a rising tide of mediocrity that threatens our very future as a nation and as a people."

The risks cited were not merely to the general fund of wisdom in the country, but to other areas as well, because education has important implications for the national psyche and the national economy. In particular, America's slim technological lead was being jeopardized.

"The risk is not only that the Japanese make automobiles more efficiently than Americans and have government subsidies for development and support. It is not just that the South Koreans recently built the world's most efficient steel mill, or that American machine tools are being displaced by German products.

"It is also that these developments signify a redistribution of trained capability throughout the globe. Knowledge, learning, information and skilled intelligence are the new raw materials of international commerce, and are today spreading throughout the world as vigorously as miracle drugs, synthetic fertilizers, and blue jeans did earlier.

"If only to keep and improve on the slim competitive edge we still retain in world markets, we must dedicate ourselves to the reform of our educational system for the benefit of all—old and young alike, affluent and poor, majority and minority."

Among the numerous signs that America's public education system is in dire straits:

—Some 23 million Americans are functionally illiterate. Among minority youth this figure is 40 percent.

—High school students score lower today on standardized tests than 26 years ago, when Sputnik was launched. In particular, Scholastic Achievement Test (SAT) scores declined every single year from 1963 to 1980. Verbal scores fell more than 50 points. Math scores fell nearly 40 points.

—American students, compared on 19 subjects with students of other industrialized nations, did not score first or second in a single instance. Americans scored last seven times.

—More than half of the students judged to be "gifted" in the U.S. don't score above average in high school. Nor do many of them perform outstandingly in later life.

—Remedial mathematics courses in U.S. colleges increased by 72 percent between 1975 and 1980. Many students enter college today despite their inability to construct a grammatically correct English sentence.

—Advanced skills among students are especially scarce. Nearly 40 percent of 17 year-olds cannot draw logical inferences from written material. Only 20 percent can write a persuasive essay. Only one third can solve a multi-step math problem.

—Scientific skills are equally lacking. Science achievement scores plummetted in this country. In 1983 they were lower than in 1977. That year they were lower than in 1973. And 1973 scores were less than scores in 1969. The world moves forward, knowledge recedes.

Many of these statistics, released by the Commission on Excellence, were previously available. But they were not widely disseminated. The reason? The chief educational organization in the United States, the National Education Association (NEA), did not want them to exist.

You see, the fact that education was in disgrace, and the NEA has been in charge of education for the last several years, leads to the inexorable conclusion: the NEA has blown it. So the NEA accused people of "emphasis on the Commission report's negative aspects, particularly the wide-spread repetition of the 'rising tide of mediocrity' catchphrase."

Of course reading the Commission on Excellence Report, it is impossible *not* to be staggered by the facts and arguments. The report is a negative statement about public education, no question about that. What is the NEA talking about?

Focus, that's what. The folks at the NEA don't want to focus on incompetent pupils, which they have managed, and incompetent teachers, whom they have represented. Instead, the NEA wants to focus on money. More money for the NEA.

"The report makes no attempt to assign blame for education's ills," according to an NEA analysis. Instead, "It takes pride in what American schools have accomplished in the past, and expresses confidence about what can be done now."

Partly true. Public education did accomplish much in the past, without the control of the NEA, and a great deal can be done about the future, if education can free itself of the shackles of the NEA.

Just how the NEA has almost single-handedly *ruined* public education will be conclusively demonstrated in this book. For now let me simply establish that there is a real problem with education, and outline its implications.

The disheartening statistics about lower test scores, lower college performance, and lower international ratings are only *symptoms* of a much larger problem. And there are other symptoms too: rising drug and alcohol consumption in school, widespread promiscuity, a declining religiosity, lack of manners and discipline in schools, and classroom vandalism.

These symptoms point to a moral-intellectual problem in America that is perhaps without precedent in 20th century history. Basically, American students are losing their ability to face the mental and moral questions that will inevitably face them in adult life. Not only are they losing the logical tools which enable them to think in later life, but they are giving up the very values that make all life worthwhile.

Thus they are plunging into a sea of ignorance and moral anarchy, buffetted by every prevailing fad, tempted by every monstrosity, whether it be Communism or hedonism, and generally incompetent to live in the great civilization which reared them with all the lavish resources at its command.

This grave problem is only now coming to the attention

of the nation's top scientists, lawyers, doctors, and intellectuals. And their usually temperate language is giving way to apocalyptic warnings.

"We are raising a generation of Americans that is scientifically and technologically illiterate," charges researcher Paul Hurd. John Slaughter, former Director of the National Science Foundation, warns of "a growing chasm between a small scientific and technological elite and a citizenry ill-informed, indeed uninformed, on issues with a scientific component."

Not just the experts, but also the general public, is crying out. Roper polls have charted the decline of confidence in the public schools. In 1959, for example, 64 percent of America felt that public education was doing a good or excellent job. In 1978 that figure was 48 percent. And in 1982 it was still lower.

The dramatic loss of public faith is best illustrated by an ABC News/*Washington Post* poll of December 1983, which showed that people have less faith in the public schools than in the two most maligned institutions of American life—the big banks, and the military.

Only 14 percent said they had a great deal of faith in public education, compared to 19 percent in banks and 32 percent in the military. Only 26 percent said they had quite a lot of faith in public education, versus 30 percent in the banks, and 34 percent in the military.

What about *lack* of faith? Well, 21 percent said they had no hope for public education; only 17 percent said that about banks, and 10 percent about the military.

Students seem to agree with these conclusions of their elders. Public school enrollment has dropped sharply over the last 15 years. This is partly accounted for by the slight drop in birth rate, following the "baby boom." But mostly it reflects a general frustration with public education. After all, most of those who bailed out of public schools ended up in the most logical place—private schools, where discipline and standards are maintained.

Public school enrollment fell from 46 million students in 1970 to 40 million in 1981, a drop of 12 percent. Meanwhile enrollment in private schools went up by 60 percent over the same period, so that there are now about 2 million students in these schools.

Nor is anybody's faith in teachers on the upswing; indeed fewer students than ever want to become teachers today. In the fall of 1982 only 4.7 percent of first-year college students said they were thinking about elementary or secondary education as a career. In 1970 that figure was 20 percent.

And of course there is the big question of whether even those 4.7 percent of college students are *competent* to teach even low-level education. Studies show that it is many times the dumb students in college, not the smart ones, who want to become teachers. Perhaps these 4.7 percent of persons are better served not teaching middle school, but *enrolled* in middle-school.

The present crop of teachers is also dissatisfied. More than one third of teachers say that if they had to do it all over again, they would not choose to teach in the public schools. In 1983 nearly 15 percent of teachers said they would definitely bail out of the profession, if given the chance; 30 percent said they would probably do so.

All these figures and complaints should suggest that education is not in a great way in this country. This is contrary to the claims of the National Education Association, which routinely tells students who will listen that they are the most sensitive and intelligent beings the planet has ever seen.

Not planet Earth, that's for sure. We all remember education the way it used to be. Now I don't want to be sentimental or nostalgic. I don't want to bring back the past, which had its own problems, racial inequality being the most acute.

But it is indisputable that public education used not to be in this desperate state, indeed it is clear that public education used to be pretty good, something we could rely on to make our children smart and decent adults, productive and honorable members of society.

It is also clear that public education achieved this with a small amount of money. Teachers have never been a highly paid lot; in fact in the past they were relatively *worse* off than they are now. This is not to say I favor paying teachers substandard wages; but it is true that despite low salaries teachers performed well in the past; from this we may conclude that high salaries are not the determinant, perhaps not even the relevant, factor in explaining teacher performance.

Consider: between 1952 and 1979, education's share of the national product more than doubled. During the same time, the number of employees in public education per 100 students increased 84 percent—from 6.8 to 12.5. Meanwhile, productivity and test scores went down.

Columnist Patrick Buchanan puts the issue in perspective: "If Boeing Company had twice as many employees as in 1952, with three times the government funding, and could not build a plane that could fly as high, fast, or far as the old B-52, would that be an argument for additional funding?"

The NEA says yes. But not because its members, having graduated from the public schools, are unable to reason. Rather, the NEA has a *vested interest* in more funds for education. So it calls for more money for itself no matter what the condition of public education.

Is education in good shape? That means we're doing well, and ought to do more of the same; give us money.

Is education in bad shape? Oh, clearly we're understaffed and underpaid. The situation can easily be turned around; give us more money.

Now assume we doubled, even tripled, salaries of all officials involved in public education. Think: how would that change things at all? We would simply be paying teachers more money. Incompetent teachers would continue to wander the corridors of our public schools, only better dressed and perhaps a little fatter. We would still have functionally illiterate children.

The "more money" solution has been hopefully and aggressively tried for the last 15 years, and it has hopelessly and spectacularly failed.

We must look elsewhere for solutions. And one place to look is our past, our history, when education, though not perfect, was better. What did we have then that we don't have now?

We had intelligent texts like the McGuffey Readers, which far from condescend to children, treated them like the adults they aspired to be. McGuffey, that wise old Episcopal preacher, knew that children's minds were not inferior to those of adults; only less developed. So McGuffey's readers included even difficult readings in small doses, and students got their Shakespeare pure.

We had dedicated teachers who loved teaching and weren't in it for the money; who loved students and weren't sleeping with them or selling them drugs; who respected the profession of teaching, instead of using it for purposes of politics and greed.

We didn't have John Dewey. That was a philosopher who knew the price of everything and the value of nothing. He was an intellectual, but he was not wise. He takes second place to the NEA in destroying public education, and he is a single man, so he must get the most per capita credit.

Admittedly Dewey's programs were exaggerated by his followers, but only in the sense that Marx's ideas were juggled by Marxists in a way that Marx might not have approved of. The point is: Dewey and Marx set education and economics respectively on potentially disastrous paths, and their pupils proved sufficient to the task of carrying those ideas to their disastrous conclusion.

One of Dewey's targets for attack was "rote learning" which the old duffer felt undermined student spontaneity and creativity. But so does brushing your teeth in the morning. Is there any other way than rote learning to memorize the multiplication tables? Or is it no longer necessary, in this progressive world, to know that two times two is four?

The point is that memory is a necessary pre-requisite to creativity. The rigor of the former enables the freedom of the latter. It is not "creative" to say that two times two is five. But once you have memorized the multiplication tables, to make a geometrical design: *that* is creative.

Another thing we had in public education that we have lost is a sense of traditional values. Some, including the NEA, say these values are "outdated." But the day values are outdated is also the day that civilization is outdated, because civilization without values is like an ocean without water.

The systematic attack on values like family, God, honesty, courage and character, which has been conducted by groups like the NEA and the liberal establishment, is in large part responsible for the chaotic state of our schools and public institutions today. This factor is possibly more important in explaining the debris of our public school system than illiterate teachers or absence of intelligent texts.

I said earlier that money was not a likely answer for education today. But I would go further: the evidence suggests that money, far from being a solution to educational problems, may in fact be the problem. After all the history of the decline of public education is also the history of increased funding for it. Perhaps there is a casual relationship between the two.

The idea that you have to fling dollars at the schools to improve them was concocted in the late 1940s, when the money was available. The Conant Report was one of the most influential documents in floating the theory that education, instead of being the selective medium it was, should become a goal for *all* Americans, regardless of their ability or vocational direction. There was some logic to this: certainly a democratic form of government presupposes an enlightened citizenry.

But public education had already begun to move away from the common-sense notions of basic knowledge and civic virtue and toward more esoteric and utilitarian goals—"social justice" causes and technical pursuits. Instead of infusing a common wisdom among our citizenry, public education has specialized and confused it, and in many cases steered it away from democracy and toward more radical forms of government, such as socialism and Communism.

These notions are suggested in some early NEA documents. In 1948 the NEA published "Education for International Understanding in American Schools" which said, "The idea has become established that the preservation of international peace and order may require that force be used to compel a nation to conduct its affairs within the framework of an established world system. The most modern expression of this doctrine and collective security is the United Nations Charter."

In one stroke, the NEA has slashed the time-honored notions of national independence, national soverignty, patriotism, and self-government in favor of what is likely to be a totalitarian World Government of the kind Orwell described in his horror classic *Nineteen Eighty Four*. For this we fought at Yorktown?

Ideas of globalism or one-worldism are still current in the NEA. As one textbook for teachers advises, "Allegiance to a nation is the biggest stumbling block to creation of international government. National boundaries and the concept of sovereignty must be abolished. The quickest way to do this is to condition the young to another and broader alliance. Opinion favorable to international government will be developed in the social studies in the elementary school."

In other words, indoctrinate the students. Not a new concept to the NEA, whose 10th Yearbook, published in 1932, said bluntly, "Conditioning is a process which may be employed by the teacher to build up attitudes in the child and predispose him to the action by which those attitudes are expressed."

So far from furthering the free and independent thought which would serve democracy so well, public education today works to control and regulate thought. It is not rote learning but rote control; students are turned into tools for political activism.

And the NEA, being in a position to influence the nation's teachers, is able to act as a control tower to manipulate our young people like robots in whatever direction they choose.

How did this parlous situation come about? The NEA has been around for 125 years, certainly not in its current destructive mode. In fact until the mid 1960s the NEA was considered a "professional association" which was a far cry from industrial unions.

The NEA was founded in 1857 to advance the cause of education, promote professional excellence, and gain recognition for the basic importance of teachers in the educational process. For more than a century it did just this, gaining widespread respect for its dignified and diligent staff and positions. Indeed largely because of NEA opposition to other union activities, like strikes, teacher unionism in general came to be thought of as apart from the militance of trade unionism.

But, as Howard Hurwitz educator and National Council for Better Education advisory board member, sadly notes, "Gone is the distinction between industrial workers and teachers as a class apart." Indeed teachers are now commonly seen picketing in jeans and torn shirts, yelling obscenities and obstructing traffic.

This "fall from grace" has in large part been due to the NEA, which has transformed itself from a sedate professional association into a militant union. The NEA of today would be unrecognizable to its past members. But images of the old NEA persist.

Columnist James Kilpatrick writes, "In some minds there may be a tendency to think of the NEA as it operated in the 1930s and 1940s. Then it was largely a home office for the federated state education associations. The national office engaged in some modest research; it lobbied some state legislators in support of higher pay and better retirement benefits. Like a middle-aged Miss Dove, it projected a good school-marmish image.

"That is long gone. These days the NEA functions as a trade union, pure and simple, as bellicose and demanding as the miners, the teamsters and the longshoremen. In the whole field of public employee unionism, few outfits are as militant—and the NEA's economic activism has been matched by an intellectual activism equally potent."

How can we respect teachers as we once did when the organization that represents them is blatantly and unapologetically political?

In 1970 NEA President Fischer said, "The NEA was identified during a Congressional debate as the second most powerful lobby in Washington. While this is the highest ranking ever given to our effectiveness, I will not be satisfied until we are the most powerful lobby."

"In 1972 NEA President Barrett announced her target of a $10 million political war chest to fight elections on behalf of the Democratic Party. Said Barrett, "Put this money with our people power, and we would not only be competitive with any existing political force, but we would be the greatest of political forces."

In 1974 NEA President Wise declared the organization's goal: "To reverse the national leadership in Washington . . . to build NEA's force over the next two years to the point where the presidential candidates will seek NEA endorsement. We have the power to elect the next President."

In 1976, after the elections, NEA President Ryor proclaimed that his groups had become "the foremost political power in the nation."

In 1980 NEA executive director Herndon declared the

NEA "a superpower of itself" and the current director Cameron has also affirmed its political character and clout.

With all this crass politicking, it is no wonder that the *New York Times* found, in May 1982, that "Teachers feel that they no longer command the respect they once did, from students, parents, and the community at large."

But the problems do not stop here. Not only is the fact that the NEA is political discouraging, but so is the *direction* of the union's politics. Quite simply, the NEA favors a socialist, anti-American politics which, if put into effect, would undermine the nation's strength, its freedom, and its values.

Also the politics of the NEA play such an obsessive role in the union today that virtually no room remains for education. So the NEA does not use politics to further educational goals; it is more accurate to say that educational goals have been displaced by politics. This is clearly evidenced by the fact that many NEA political goals—such as its support for a nuclear "freeze" or abortion—have nothing to do with education.

Indeed, the NEA's support for certain political ends—legalization of marijuana, for instance—would add to and complicate existing problems with public education.

Says Scott Thompson, executive director of the National Association of Secondary School Principals, writing in *Phi Delta Kappan,* a prestigious education journal, "The NEA no longer contributes significantly to the improvement of teaching and learning for students. It looks after the narrow interests of its members rather than after the broader interests of its constituency." And even the NEA's utility to its own members is dubious, as I will show.

It is a bit hard for parents and the public to understand how a single group, even a lobby as militant as the NEA, could have played such a large role in the ruin of the American public school system. But the facts are irrefutable, the danger is clear and present, and if we remain apathetic the tragedy will continue, with consequences unimagineable and probably irreparable for our society.

Representative John Ashbrook (R-Ohio) said of the NEA, "I think there's a growing concern that the NEA's priorities these days break down like this—power first, politics second, education third."

Ashbrook was being cautious. It is probably more accurate to say that the NEA's priority today is power and politics, indeed power politics. Education counts little or not at all.

Take a look at this telegram which the NEA recently sent to U.S. Senators. It is quoted in full:

To: All members of the U.S. Senate

From: Linda Tarr-Whelan

Director, Government Relations

National Education Association

On behalf of NEA's 1.7 million members, I urge you to oppose S.J. Res. 3, a constitutional amendment to ban abortions.

NEA believes that reproductive freedom is one of the most fundamental human and civil rights. The decision about abortions is an economic one for millions of American working women and their families. Whether or not a woman chooses to have a child is a matter for her to decide, based on imput from her family, her doctor & her pastor—not the government.

NEA considers reproductive freedom of choice the constitutional right of every woman and strongly opposes any amendment to the constitution or statute which would limit or eradicate this right.

End message.

Now, we should ask: what is the NEA doing sending urgent cables to the U.S. Senate about abortion? In what way is abortion connected to the issue of education? The word "education" was not mentioned once in the cable.

This cable could be dismissed as the malevolent work of some NEA official who felt very strongly about abortion and used the organization to propagate his or her views. But radical politicking of this sort has become the norm, not the exception, at the NEA. Indeed it dominates the work of this union.

Consider this entry from the *Virginia Journal of Education,* published by the state arm of the NEA:

"Send a birthday card to Dr Martin Luther King, Jr on January 15.

"That's what the minority affairs committee of the Richmond Education Association is urging local associations to do.

"'We want to call attention to his birthday and to help get a bill passed to make it a holiday in Virginia,' says Lola Gilkes, who chairs the committee.

"Letters have been sent out to local association presidents asking them to send birthday cards to Dr King in care of the local NEA. Richmond teachers are also working with churches and other organizations in their area."

All this was before Martin Luther King's birthday was declared a national holiday. And because of efforts like this, it was.

Now I don't object to anyone celebrating anyone else's birthday. But the NEA chose the occasion to lobby for a bill that was clearly controversial, that divided the American public, that NEA members could not speak their minds about—because they were not consulted.

The NEA can bypass its members in this way because it is not set up as a democratic organization. Local elections are held, but like in the Soviet Union, they are strictly "token" elections. Locally elected representatives have no real power; virtually all of their decisions can be vetoed by the national office.

So the rank and file members of the NEA have been cut off from the rest of society by the NEA bureaucrats. It is sort of an intellectual isolation. Teachers are deprived of their power, while the NEA, masquerading as a teachers' representative, controls the lives of teachers and of school children.

The agenda of the NEA is set by a small and radical band of activists. They are accountable to nobody but themselves. They have gigantic budgets to work with. And they are steering the NEA in the direction of making it a revolutionary organ that Marx would have been proud of.

The leftist politics of the NEA should be seen in the context of the origins and growth of public education in America. Economist Milton Friedman calls education "the only bastion of socialism in a sea of free enterprise in America."

Indeed education is our only major national project which is almost entirely under state and federal control. How did this come to be?

Our forefathers were hostile to the idea of the government controlling their lives. In the late 18th century Thomas Jefferson could not persuade the state of Virginia to provide even as little as three years of elementary education at public expense.

The first public school was opened in 1821 in Boston. It

provided three years of free instruction in English, mathematics, geography, and religion. The purpose of these early public (or common) schools was primarily to transfer the Calvinist Puritan religion from one generation to the next.

Indeed private schools grew as the nation's economy grew more prosperous and there was a need for education that was less geared toward religion and more towards practical matters.

This is ironic in view of the fact that private schools today provide religious and moral education, and the public schools have rejected any concept of faith and ethics altogether.

It is widely claimed that public schools were necessary because previously only a small and elite segment of the population was receving private education. Not true.

Studies show that nearly 90 percent of children attended school, despite the fact that they had to pay small sums to do so, and despite the fact that there were no compulsory attendance laws in effect, as there are today.

The promoters of public education sought not to promote the Calvinist faith, as did the original founders of public schools, but instead to destroy private education, which they viewed as a tool of capitalism.

The first organized effort against private schools came around 1818, and was led by Robert Owen, a self-proclaimed socialist who rejected the notion that man improves his lot by himself. Rather, Owen believed, it is society and education which should do things *for* him.

The idea that man is perfectible through education later came to be embedded in a larger, more honest, American myth: that we seek a strong, opportunity society in which rich and poor alike will prosper. Education is viewed as an important means to that end.

But the socialists knew that private education was bringing about prosperity with equal speed. Their objection to private control was, therefore, ideological and not practical.

Also they realized that education that was privately controlled would not be subject to indoctrination from any one source. On the other hand public controlled education would be easily manipulated. Owen and his followers wanted to manipulate it in the direction of socialism.

This is not to claim that all those who support public education today are socialists. Indeed I count myself among the supporters of public education. If I didn't care deeply about it, I would not be writing this book about the NEA, which I feel is ruining public education. I hope to arrest the decline of public education, which is losing ground very fast to private education these days.

I simply want to point out that public education was, from the outset, a vehicle of socialists to impose their will upon the American people, and even today there is a strong socialist presence in education, as evidenced by the strong influence of socialism on the NEA. There are some who will object to my using such strong terms as "socialist." These terms may bother some liberals, but they do not bother the officials who freely call themselves socialists or at least admit that their programs are based on socialist principles. There was a time when critics of the NEA didn't dare call the union socialist—until the NEA itself embraced socialism. Now we are a step further: there are many who don't dare call the NEA 'Marxist'—a kind of reverse McCarthyism has evolved. But, as we shall see, there are many Marxist sympathizers in the NEA apparatus, and several NEA policies are based on Marxist principles.

Communists began to infiltrate the NEA in the mid 1930s, as is clear from this statement by Richard Frank in *Communist,* a Party publication: "In the effort to organize the teachers, every care must be taken to bring together in united front actions all existing teachers organizations. Special attention must be paid to secure such action with the American Association of University Professors, the National Education Association (NEA), and the Guild. Our party members *in these organizations* must work actively toward that end." (Emphasis added.)

A bit earlier, in 1932, Communist organizer William Z. Foster wrote in *Towards a Soviet America,* "The schools, colleges and universities will be coordinated and grouped under the National Department of Education and its state and local branches."

Socialists and Communists in the NEA applied themselves toward a single goal for education: the displacement of "quality" by "equality."

Columnist Patrick Buchanan writes, "What happened to American education is that, about a quarter century ago, the idea of excellence was displaced by the egalitarian ethic. Equality of funding for schools and the racial composition of the classroom became more vital considerations than whether learning was taking place."

It is a matter of great philosophical dispute whether it is possible to have quality and equality in anything. After all quality is achieved only when there is opportunity, or liberty; while equality almost always means the squashing of liberty.

For years Americans tried to resolve this conflict by touting the idea of "equality of opportunity." This slogan con-

42

tained both the ideas of freedom and egalitarianism. Everybody was to be given a chance to succeed freely. But it is not a long distance from equality of opportunity to equality of *result*. And the NEA has taken that road. Today excellence means nothing to the radical union, as is clear from its opposition to almost all tests, which it brands "racist," "biased," and "destructive."

What means a great deal to the NEA today is social activism. And education is only important to the extent that it is a means to social, or perhaps more accurately socialist, goals.

We should not underestimate the appeal of socialist ideas in our country. Just because this is a democratic capitalist country does not mean all traces of competing ideologies have been eradicated. Of course socialism is a bad word in America, but then socialists seldom use it. They call themselves "liberals." Or, more tellingly, they say they "reject labels."

Socialism is appealing to some because it promises a perfect society, a Utopia, a heaven on earth. This is something Christianity only promises for the next world. But socialists say you can have it here, right now. Taste of the socialist apple and you can be like God. As you know, the apple in the garden of Eden was very red and luscious.

Jean Francois-Revel once wrote, "They judge socialism by its promise, but fascism by its record." Unlike fascism, socialism does not submit itself to refutation by empirical data. No matter that socialism has utterly ruined many countries, no matter that its influences have corroded education in America, socialists continue to work for their goals with undiminished enthusiasm. They regard all failures of socialism as "deviations" from true socialism. This makes them very dangerous, because there is no stopping the evils

43

they would inflict upon us en route to the elusive, never-witnessed true socialism.

Today the NEA is not imprudent enough to use socialist rhetoric, but it was not always so astute politically. In 1937 the NEA Report of the Secretary said candidly, "Education should and can be made a force to equalize the conditions of men."

Conditions? Notice that we have already gone from equality of opportunity to equality of result. Not only should all children start the race equal, but they must all finish at the same time too.

Socialist tendencies in the NEA did not restrict themselves to seeking socialism in this country, but extended themselves to global egalitarianism. From the 1941 Report of the NEA Secretary:

"The schools should give serious curriculum consideration to the problems of post-war reconstruction, including a future world organization based on democratic federal union."

All this is not merely past history. Indeed as I said earlier the NEA has become *more* aggressive, more militant, and more radical about its politics than at any previous point in its history.

It seldom admits this, of course. NEA presidents continue to call the group a professional association dedicated to quality teaching. But as the saying goes, if it walks and quacks like a duck, chances are it is a duck.

The NEA is a radical union, no question about it. And it is a union hardly concerned about genuine questions of education. This was as much as conceded by the Oregon branch of the NEA. Its Lane County UNISERV declared in a bulletin:

"The major purpose of our association is not the education of children, rather it is or ought to be the extension and/or preservation of our members' rights. We earnestly care about the kids and learning, but that is secondary to the other goals."

What teacher can achieve results by saying, "We care about the kids but . . ."? The Oregon Educational Association has exploded the myth of the NEA as a pro-education group. It claims instead that the NEA is a teachers' union.

Later we will inquire how the NEA represents even its member teachers. For now let us just notice that 40 percent of NEA members are Republicans. Many of them probably vote conservative; in fact, it is estimated that 50 percent of NEA members voted for President Reagan in 1980.

If the NEA truly represents teachers, why would it promote an aggressively radical political program which most of its members cannot agree with? And why would it risk its credibility in educational circles by fighting for issues only tangentially, if at all, related to education? What stake do its members have in these peripheral issues? How can they appreciate their dues going toward these radical proposals?

Before the 98th Congress of the United States convened, the NEA drew up a legislative agenda which it lobbied for. This called for the following:

—One third of public education should be federally funded.

—The government should guarantee teachers collective bargaining rights which the NEA would be in charge of enforcing.

—Congress should pass the Equal Rights Amendment (ERA).

—Congress should not impose any restrictions on forced busing.

—No defense increases should be approved.

—The Kennedy-Hatfield nuclear freeze proposal which would restrict the U.S. defense build-up should be supported.

—Tuition tax credits and vouchers should be voted down because they help private schools.

—Right to work laws which undermine the NEA's monopoly over teachers' rights should be voted down.

—Income tax indexing, which would give working people protection against inflation, should be repealed.

—Oil companies should not be permitted to look for alternate areas of energy development.

—Gas deregulation should be opposed.

—Martin Luther King's birthday should be a national holiday.

—Support should be extended to Asian-Pacific Heritage Week sponsored by the NEA.

—Smoking should be banned in public places.

—Bilingual programs should not be opposed.

—The U.S. should not aid the democratic government in El Salvador but should not oppose the Sandinista junta in Nicaragua.

And so on. You will notice that only a couple of these proposals concern education, and they are so radical and preposterous that the NEA probably knew that they had no chance of being passed.

For example the NEA knew that only 7-9 percent of education is funded currently by the federal government. For the NEA to expect one third to be federally bankrolled was outside the realm of possibility.

So also collective bargaining laws are passed by states. Many states already permit teachers to bargain collectively. The NEA claim that not only should the federal government intervene in this, but that it should appoint the NEA as the legitimate bargaining agent on behalf of teachers was a naked, and implausible, grab for power.

The published NEA legislative agenda noted that "the lobbying effort for the 98th Congress will be pursued vigorously in Washington and in each state to work toward the achievement of NEA policy goals and, in the process, to define clearly which Senators and Representatives are friends of education."

The implication is that those who don't accept the NEA's drive for monopoly control of education, and its leftist political goals, are not "friends of education."

What are some of these leftist political goals? The NEA agenda states them clearly:

"Any efforts to expand sectarian practices in the schools; to limit the jurisdiction of the federal courts; to eliminate reproductive freedom; to eliminate busing as a desegregation alternative available to the courts; or to weaken affirmative action programs to correct historic racial, sexual, or age discrimination; to intern or contain any racially identifiable segments of our society must be opposed."

This statement, couched in civil rights rhetoric, is actually a call for forced busing, reverse discrimination, abortion on demand, and special treatment for homosexuals.

Another goal of the NEA:

"NEA supports the concept of the Kennedy-Hatfield nuclear arms freeze resolution as introduced in the 97th Congress. Immediate strategic arms control should include a complete halt in the nuclear arms race through mutual and verifiable cessation of testing, production, and further deployment of nuclear delivery systems and other destabilizing weapons."

Again this statement, which seems innocuous, is in fact a blatant political gambit. The NEA knows very little about defense issues—and I'm not blaming it; it's a teachers union, not the Arms Control Agency. So it is not surprising that the NEA does not understand the serious difficulties attached to a "mutual, verifiable" freeze.

Other statements by the NEA indicate that it doesn't really care about the "mutual" and "verifiable" aspects of the freeze. It just wants the U.S. to disarm. It uses the inclusive rhetoric of the joint freeze to seem bipartisan. But in fact it knows that its lobbying has no effect whatsoever on the foreign policy of the Soviet Union. Nor does it want to. It's not Soviet weapons which worry the NEA, it's American weapons. Even though it is not American but Soviet weapons which will destroy the American lives the NEA professes to be concerned about.

How do we know that the NEA doesn't care about Soviet atrocities? Well, the NEA routinely makes statements about human rights violations around the globe. It has frequently chastized such abuses in the Phillipines, Chile, Honduras, El Salvador, and South Africa.

But the NEA has almost never criticized the infinitely more barbaric practices of the Soviet Union. It is unusually laconic about documenting or lamenting murder and mayhem by Soviet client states.

Remember, the Soviet Union is a country which muzzles its press, puts political dissidents in jail, persecutes Jews and Christians, throws its genuine pacifists and indeed dissidents of all kinds in concentration camps. It has killed between 30 and 50 million of its own people, five times the number of Jews Hitler killed during World War II.

Yet the NEA behaves as though the U.S. was the villain in the superpower struggle, even though the U.S. has not done anything even remotely resembling Soviet barbarism. The U.S. is reluctantly involved in its struggle with the Soviet Union, it is a defensive struggle, and it is aimed at protecting the freedom of American citizens.

One important freedom that U.S. foreign policy seeks to secure is the freedom of unions to organize. But the NEA insists on attacking the very system that makes its existence possible, while ignoring the evils of the system which would shatter and persecute it.

As Eric Hoffer said, "He who bites the hand that feeds him, also licks the boot that kicks him." This is aptly applied to the NEA.

One reason given for the reticence of the NEA in criticizing the Soviet Union is alleged Soviet influence in the NEA. I will devote a chapter to examining the connections between the NEA and far-left, including Communist, groups. These connections are myriad.

For now let me simply show that the NEA actively employs Marxist tactics and Marxist rhetoric in its lobbying strategy. A report was submitted to the NEA by J. Michael Arisman, in which he summarized the views of three strategists for the Industrial Areas Foundation: Saul Alinsky, Edward Chambers, and Richard Harmon. Many items in this report have become standard NEA practice.

The central concept of the Alinsky Report is "power." Says Alinsky bluntly, "What if teachers don't want power? Organize the ones who do."

So right from the start the goal is established: not representation of teachers, but political power.

Power is easily built around a leader. What kind of leader is sought? "The building of a power base needs a leader, who is initially more important than the number of people you have behind him," the report says. "Among others, Martin Luther King, Ho Chi Minh, and Fidel Castro suggest the wisdom of this advice."

The role models for the NEA have been announced. One of them is a genuine civil rights leader, but the other two are Communists. Ho Chi Minh is responsible for the deaths of many American boys in South East Asia; perhaps this is why he appeals to the folks at the NEA, who aren't big on the military.

How to use power? Says the Alinsky Report, "After each meeting make a 3 by 5 card indicating the person's self interest, relationships with existing institutions, relationships with other people and what type of 'action' they have been in previously. i.e. civil rights demonstrations."

Now perhaps this is intended to help public relations, but is it also intended as a blackmail weapon?

The latter notion becomes more likely when you see that Alinsky is interested not in working with people to advance their interests and solve problems, but in generating confrontation.

"Alinsky would not recommend exchanges of letters or private discussions with the superintendent as a way of building the organization. Such meetings or such correspondence might solve the problem, but they would not provide the kind of action that is exciting and what makes your people want to get involved with the organization to participate. Going to court is likewise a local anesthetic; it freezes the action."

Instead, "You must seize upon the development of the other side's tactics. This corresponds to the idea of training people by making the other side insult or assault your people so that they can learn what the other side is really like. In fact, getting the superintendent to insult or to assault

50

your people is regarded as of higher value than ten weeks of formal training."

It's power over reform, all right. Concludes Alinsky, "It is hard to deal with an enemy with whom you have a personal relationship. You should not let your people fraternize with the enemy. Distance helps to polarize the issue . . . The organizer must not resolve issues even though he might be able to."

This rhetoric is very similar to that of the uncompromising Marxists. It has all the ingredients: surliness, inhumanity, an affinity for violence, a hatred of authority no matter what its source.

All this makes the political activity of the NEA, which comprises the majority of its activity, extremely dangerous. NEA politics extends to all areas of our lives. The union even agitates for such trivial issues as changing to the metric system.

Where do genuine educational issues—such as teacher competence, a safe and serious academic environment, parent-teacher relationships, the availability of advanced courses, the question of how to teach values, and so on— fit into the NEA mosaic?

Answer: they aren't very important to the NEA. Where the union does take a stand, it is to favor the expansion of its own centralized power, which is not the power of its member teachers, but the power of its bureaucratic and unelected staff in Washington.

It's a sordid situation, but so far you've only seen the tip of the iceberg.

CHAPTER
4

Although the NEA admits it is political, it denies that it is a far-left union which wants to impose socialism and internationalism in the American people.

But what does the evidence say? Let us look at some of the statements of NEA officials, current and former; let us examine some of the events the NEA has sponsored and attended; let us hear what socialist and Communist groups say about the NEA.

William Foster, former national chairman of the Communist Party (CPUSA), wrote in *Toward A Soviet America* that he wanted the "cultural revolution" to be advanced under the aegis of a national Department of Education (DOE).

Ironically that is exactly what the NEA lobbied for during the 1976 presidential campaign, and a DOE is exactly what Jimmy Carter gave the union in gratitude for its support.

Foster wrote that the DOE should be "revolutionized, cleaned of religious, patriotic and other features of the bourgeois ideology. The students will be taught on the basis of Marxian dialectical materialism, internationalism, and the general ethics of the new Socialist society."

Now this is what Foster wanted for the DOE, but is this what the NEA wants for it?

The March-April 1976 issue of *Today's Education,* an NEA publication, printed an article titled "A Declaration of Interdependence" written by one-world proponent Henry Steele Commager.

Among the things Commager said:

"Now we must join with others to bring forth a new world order.

"It is essential that mankind free itself from the limitations of national prejudice. (He means patriotism.)

"All people are part of one global community.

"We call upon all nations to strengthen and sustain the United Nations and its specialized agencies, and other institutions of world order, and to broaden the jurisdiction of the World Court."

Some of this seems innocent enough, but not when you know what the NEA knows full well, that the United Nations is dominated, if not completely controlled, by the Soviet Union and its satellites.

The NEA is calling for the U.S. literally to surrender its independence to the Soviet run UN. And it audaciously prints this article in the Bicentennial year of American independence; which I think is a real insult to those brave men and women who died so that America could be free.

No wonder that columnist Russell Evans wrote in 1983:

"A big wheel in the machinery of the proposed New World Order is the National Education Association, now enjoying its crowning achievement: the Cabinet-level Department of Education. In the master plan for this New World Order, a scheme that is frightening more and more Americans, it appears that the NEA wants to control education; the Federal Reserve wants to control the currency; the Trilateral Commission wants to control the economy; the National Council of Churches wants to control religion. This is an insidious global machine designed to crush our national soverignty."

Perhaps Evans is being a bit alarmist, but he is justified in his claims about the NEA.

In 1908 the NEA passed a resolution which said, "The public high schools should not be fitting schools for higher institutions . . . The high schools must become the poor man's colleges."

Now I do not deny that the poor as well as the rich should avail themselves of public education. But the NEA formulation is unmistakeably Marxist in its pitting the rich against the poor.

In 1937 the NEA declared in its 15th Yearbook, Department of Superintendence:

"The present capitalistic and nationalistic school system has been supplanted in but one place—Russia—and that change was effected by revolution. Hence the verdict of history would seem to indicate that we are likely to have to depend upon revolution for social change of an important and far-reaching character."

This Marxist interpretation was extended into the 1960s, when an NEA brochure "The Root of Opposition to Federal Aid to Education" noted:

"Under the surface, in reality, it is an economic battle— the classic pattern of historic battles between the haves and the have-nots, between those who control the wealth of the land and those who make up the masses."

The brochure continued, "It is not popular, or even polite, to describe it in these terms. We are all brainwashed from childhood to pretend that the United States has no classes or masses. We are all supposed to be Americans, believing that capitalism and free enterprise came down to us on stone tablets from the mountain."

The NEA's attack on free enterprise is only a part of its leftist crusade. It also routinely attacks patriotism, American defense policy, religion, and morality.

Atheist groups have not ignored the wooing sounds coming from the NEA. The anti-religious magazine *The Humanist,* for example, printed in its February 1983 issue an article called "A Religion for a New Age" by John Dunphy. He wrote:

"I am convinced that the battle for humankind's future must be waged and won *in the public school classroom* by teachers who correctly perceive their role as the proselytizers of a new faith; a religion of humanity that recognizes and respects what theologians call divinity in every human being."

Notice terms "new faith" and "religion of humanity" which denote that we are talking about the humanist religion here, the very humanism that is said to be a bogeyman of right-wingers and evangelicals. Yes Virginia, humanism exists as a religion, and it is making its way into the public schools.

And what about Christianity? Dunphy believes that it should perish in a class-conflict with humanism.

"The classrooms must and will become an arena of conflict between the old and the new—the rotting corpse of Christianity, together with all its adjacent misery, and the new faith of Humanism, resplendent in its promise of a world in which the never-realized Christian idea of 'love thy neighbour' will finally be achieved."

This is the NEA's final goal for America: a public school system in which Christian values are trampled on and eradicated, in which humanism reigns supreme, in which standards of excellence and character give way to standards of egalitarianism and minority rule, in which patriotism and national pride are destroyed in favor of globalism and internationalism, where the U.S. bows down to the Soviet rigged consensus in the United Nations.

Is that what you want for your children? The death of

America? Because I firmly believe that that would be the result of the NEA achieving its objectives.

Phil Keisling wrote in the respected liberal publication *The Washington Monthly,* "If Marx and Engels were living in today's America, they would be writing *The Education Manifesto.* Millions of our citizens are being oppressed, not by the evils of the capitalist system, but by a public school system that is bad and getting worse."

I do not mean to say that the NEA is deliberately ruining the schools, that it wants the schools ruined. In fact, as I said earlier, the NEA doesn't care about the schools. It only wants power and political objectives.

But it is convenient for the NEA that the effects of the various policies it supports are to degrade and ruin the public school system in America. Because, then, as Keisling notes, an atmosphere of frustration and repression is created out of which the NEA's goal of revolution may result.

A review of documents put out by the Communist Party in the United States and related socialist and far-left groups shows that these people realize that they have an ally in the NEA.

They also realize that the way for Communism to achieve power in the U.S. is not by working independently, outside the two-party apparatus, for change, but rather for Communists and Stalinists to work within the Democratic Party. Since the NEA is also working entirely within the Democratic Party, this makes for real chumminess between education officials and far-left organizers.

Gus Hall, the infamous American Communist, writes in *Political Affairs,* described as a "theoretical journal of the Communist Party USA," that the CPUSA should work with radical candidates in the Democratic Party.

"It is clear that there will be many more candidates

running, starting with the Democratic primaries, who will not fit into the lesser-evil slot. They will include many more Afro-American and hopefully many labor candidates.

"The time element (for revolution) calls for broad-based, ad hoc electoral coalitions, coalitions that will work to run and elect anti-Reagan candidates, starting with the Democratic primaries, especially in the races for House and Senate seats."

Previously the Communists had attacked the Democratic Party, which they termed a "lesser evil" perhaps worth voting for but certainly not worthy of strong support.

Now Gus Hall changes his tune: the Democrats, particularly far-left Democrats, aren't that much out of line with Communist thinking.

"Lesser evil was never meant to be a blanket cover-all designation for all Democrats for all time," writes Hall. "For instance members of the Congressional Black Caucus and a number of trade union leaders who run and get elected on the Democratic Party line do not fit into the lesser-evil box."

The CPUSA has developed a coalition strategy which Hall phrases thus: "Communists should be careful not to appear to be in any way dividing, rather than uniting, those who are against the Reagan forces."

Education is an important part of the anti-Reagan coalition. The NEA itself admits this over and over. It classifies Reagan as an "enemy of education." That is because he refuses to be pals with the kind of people who are popular over at the NEA: Gus Hall and his comrades.

Interestingly Hall sees his alliance with groups like the trade unions and the NEA as "a major opportunity to mobilize the whole party to speak to millions through radio,

TV, newspapers, speaking on campuses, at rallies and press conferences, and by issuing our own electoral material."

Hall predicts that Reagan will be defeated in 1984 by a revolutionary "mass wave that will mainly express itself through the Democratic Party and especially during the primary campaigns."

As an example of the success of coalitions containing Communists and others in the Democratic Party, Hall proudly cites the march by 500,000 people in New York in June 1982 which he calls "a mile stone for the movement for peace and sanity in our time."

I don't know about sanity, but the peace Hall is referring to is the peace of the grave. Because that will be the fate of the U.S. if it succumbs to the power of the Soviet Union.

How important a role does the NEA play in this Democratic Party-Communist Party coalition?

I quote directly from an article written in *Political Affairs* by Tim Wheeler, who is also a writer for the *Daily World,* a Communist party newspaper. Wheeler says:

"The Communist Party candidates for President and vice president will be a powerful voice in the elections, putting forward a genuine alternative to Reaganism, and will play a unifying role in the anti-Reagan movement. In the course of this struggle, the Communist Party will emerge as a stronger force fighting for the unity of the working class and all oppressed people of the United States, and for an end to exploitation and all the evils of war and racism, through a socialist government that will plan the social, political and economic life of the nation for the benefit of all."

Immediately following this is a description of the New Coalition that the Communists will help build, after which is noted:

"The National Education Association has contributed office space in its headquarters building in Washington."

Pardon? Did you say the NEA is giving office space to Communists to help organize an anti-Reagan coalition to bring socialism and maybe Communism to the United States?

The conclusion is unavoidable. The NEA is indeed in cahoots with these subversives and revolutionaries. It has never once criticized them, at any rate.

A series of teacher union exchanges sponsored by the NEA is very illustrative of its attitude towards Communism and the Soviet Union. Over the last several years, according to NEA literature, the NEA has received several delegations from the government-controlled, so-called "teacher unions" of the Soviet Union.

The NEA has praised these unions and presented their representatives to teachers and to the press in the U.S. as legitimate representatives of teachers in the Soviet Union.

In 1979 the NEA reciprocated by sending an official delegation to the Soviet Union, to meet with Soviet "teacher unions." The Soviet news agency Tass used the occasion for a massive propaganda victory, telling its citizens that the fact that free unions in the U.S. recognized unions in Russia means that unions in Russia must be free.

"The members of the U.S. NEA delegation were able to exchange opinions with their Soviet colleagues on problems of educating the younger generation, and to see for themselves the specific achievement of the Soviets in these fields," reported Tass.

When the Soviets send their stooges, probably KGB officers in teachers's guise, to the U.S. the NEA congratulated them. The NEA submitted Soviet officials to the U.S. press for interviews. Indeed the NEA's own magazine featured an interview with Tamara Yanushkovskaya, whom it described as the "USSR's Teacher Union President."

The article, which was distributed to more than a million teachers and households, allowed Yanushkovskaya to set forth Soviet propaganda on how well Russian schools are doing, how there is freedom and an atmosphere of open discussion, how there is religious freedom.

Yanushkovskaya even said, "According to the demands of Soviet legislation, the demands of the trade unions must be met."

Is that why free trade unionists in the Soviet Union are sent to jail? Of course the demands of official unions are met, because they coincide with official policy. Are they representative of the Soviet worker, of Soviet people? Of course not.

In Communist countries free trade unions are illegal. (That is why Lech Walesa was imprisoned and is harassed by the Polish government.) The government establishes "unions" but they are simply extentions of the arm of the government. They enforce the production quotas set by the government. They are not permitted to deviate from Soviet policy.

What a disgrace for the NEA to treat these unions as legitimate and give them such publicity. What a disgrace for the NEA to fawn before the Soviet unions. Does it prefer to kiss the Soviet boot than to operate freely under the democratic system in this country? Would NEA officials prefer to be mouthpieces for official U.S. policy? Then they would have to sing the praises of the very Ronald Reagan they hate.

By contrast with the NEA, it should be said that the American Federation of Teachers, despite its left-wing politics, nevertheless refuses to acknowledge Soviet unions or phony unions in other Communist countries. It has urged the

NEA to cut off its ties with these so-called unions and stop receiving Soviet and Cuban officials.

But in this the AFT is like the parent who asks his daughter to stop seeing the car thief. She cannot; her heart has been lost to him. So also the NEA refuses to stop receiving representatives from Russia and Cuba. They represent the vision of the future for the NEA, I suppose.

In 1934 Willard Givens issued a report at the NEA's Department of Superintendence which said that "Many drastic changes must be made. A dying laissez faire must be completely destroyed and all of us, including the owners, must be subjected to a large degree of social control."

The NEA doesn't make statements quite as inflammatory, but its actions speak louder than words. At its 1978 convention in Dallas, for example, the NEA vocally supported the attempt of Hector Marroquin to remain in the U.S.

Marroquin is a Communist terrorist wanted in Mexico for crimes against the state. Then he was a member of the Socialist Workers' Party, an arm of the Trotskyite Communists.

When NEA vice president Willard McGuire announced passage of the proposal calling for Marroquin's visa clearance, several hundred NEA officials applauded. Revolutionary Communism has its adherents in the U.S.

Marroquin confirmed this: "Angela Davis has supported me, members of the Communist Party have supported my cause."

Many of these heinous NEA activities were sponsored under the direction of NEA executive director Terry Herndon, who describes himself as a "left-wing Democrat."

In 1979 Herndon had the NEA give its official endorsement to a TV series called "The Unknown War." So biased and propagandistic was this "documentary" that even the *New York Times* screamed foul.

The *Times* said the series "distorts by omission, oversimplification and half truth. 'The Unknown War' is soft-core propaganda rather than an attempt to arrive at historic truth. Nothing makes this clearer than the fact that it is scheduled to be shown unaltered early next year on Soviet television."

Albert Shanker, president of the American Federation of Teachers, said 'The Unknown War' was a disgraceful pro-Soviet movie. "The first program sets the stage by telling us that in the 1930s the quality of life in the Soviet Union was improving. There is no mention of the forced collectivization which resulted in the deaths of more than 10 million Ukranian and Russian peasants from 1931 to 1933, nothing of the purge trials, no awareness of the Gulag Archipelago. The series defends the Hitler-Stalin pact as a clever ploy to buy time to prepare for war—a theory which does not conform to historical evidence available. The Soviet invasion of Poland in 1939 is whitewashed as a move to reclaim land seized by Poland eighteen years earlier. Lithuania, Latvia and Estonia go unmentioned."

My own suspicion is that the NEA is so friendly toward Soviet totalitarianism because it sees that any opposition to the Soviet Union would stand in the way of its goal of a collectivized world government. I think the NEA wants this above all else. It would do away with our present system at all costs; it wants a benign world order, if possible; a Soviet-controlled totalitarian world order, if necessary.

And the NEA has designed its own internal apparatus to conform to these centralized-rule guidelines. Gordon Drake of the Christian Crusade complains that the NEA has created a school system in which "our children are being indoctrinated for a new collectivist world government."

This leads journalist Allan Stang to cry angrily, "The most important difference between Mussolini's system and the NEA's system is that Herndon's English is better than his Italian."

Not so funny.

The NEA is a teachers' organization. Not only does it claim to represent its 1.8 million members, but indeed the interests of all teachers and of education in general.

But is this so? Recently the NEA sued a teacher at a local Bible college for responding to an article in the Bristol Courier in Tennessee by Virginia Education Association president Walt Mica and NEA director Terry Herndon. Mrs Clark, the teacher, was sued for $100,000 for quoting NEA material which advocated one-worldism, values clarification, and sexual license.

Chalk up another one for free speech. Also let it dispel the myth that the NEA stands for all teachers, and for education in general. The NEA stands for its own private power, and in many cases that is opposed to the general interest.

If the NEA stood for the interests of all teachers, why would it impose on them a system of forced dues? Why doesn't it make membership in the NEA truly voluntary? The NEA has tried to institute a system by which money is automatically deducted from teachers' salaries to fund NEA political activity. Those teachers who didn't want to pay would have to file written forms with the NEA to get their own money back. This is called the "negative check off system."

What a ripoff. From 1974 through 1977 the NEA collected millions of dollars this way. An intrepid teacher sued, and Judge Gasch of the U.S. District Court quoted the NEA's attorney as follows:

"It is well recognized that if you take away the mechanism of payroll deduction you won't collect a penny from these people, and it has nothing to do with voluntary or involuntary. I think it has to do with the nature of the beast, and the beasts who are our teachers who are dispersed all over cities who simply don't come up with money regardless of the purpose."

Congratulations, teachers. You have just been called "beasts" by the NEA. But it shouldn't be surprising, really. The NEA has treated teachers as mute animals, with little say in the running of the union, for many years now. Indeed, I will show later, the NEA has held the great majority of teachers in contempt and condescension.

If the NEA truly represented teachers, and fought for their interests, wouldn't teachers find it worthwhile to pay a small fraction of their salary to keep the NEA working for them?

The fact is that the NEA knows that it no longer operates in the interests of teachers, it has its own hidden agenda, which many if not most teachers may find repulsive. So the NEA, in the tradition of all totalitarian systems, tries to forcibly extract money from teachers. Compulsory dues.

The "negative check off system" of raising money was developed by radical activist Ralph Nader, who raised money for his "Public Interest Research Groups" devoted to radical pursuits from students on campuses. Last year Nader asked Congress to pass legislation cutting off federal money to private and public colleges which refuse to endorse his negative check-off contribution scheme. In the name of the "public interest" these totalitarians are trying to wrap their tentacles around our society and choke off its freedom.

The reason the negative check-off is a profitable fund raising system is that while in theory it is possible to write the NEA and get your money back, it is frequently a cumbersome process to do so. Many teachers don't bother. Others may not even know that their paycheck is being tampered with to bankroll the militant NEA. One usually assumes that when one gets a salary check, only taxes have eaten into the amount. Not everyone knows of the NEA ripoff scheme—and indeed that's the best way to commit theft: not even the victim knows he or she has been had.

Said Thomas Harris, former chairman of the Federal Election Commission, who was for many years attorney for the AFL-CIO, of the NEA negative check off plan:

"The particular device here proposed or here used by the NEA is, in fact, one that has been familiar to union lawyers for some thirty years. No other union has conceived that it was permissible either under the 1947 Taft-Hartley Act or under the subsequent revisions."

Not only is the NEA scheme arrogant, it is illegal. And it has been the source for a great deal of suffering among many teachers.

Through negative checkoff and monopoly bargaining rights the NEA seeks to dominate the professional lives of teachers. It builds its own power by smashing the careers of teachers who resist the NEA, and working for large monies for teachers who mouth the official NEA line.

Take the case of Susan LaVine, a tenured Illinois educator who was evaluated thus by her school supervisor:

"I need an entirely new list of superlatives to express adequately my professional and personal opinion of her.

She is an outstanding teacher. Her students love her and learn from her."

A few months later, Susan LaVine was fired from her job. The reason? The town had signed a contract imposing compulsory NEA membership on the teachers. Susan La-Vine, being an independent sort, refused to join.

So union officials pressured school administrators and the school board to charge LaVine with "deficient and unsatisfactory performance as a teacher."

Upon her dismissal, LaVine said succinctly, "I just strongly feel that no one should be fired for reasons other than quality."

But the NEA doesn't care about quality. The NEA cares about the NEA. So outstanding teacher LaVine became a casualty of the NEA's drive for monopoly control.

So did Charleen Sciambi, a California teacher who won the 1983 Outstanding Foreign Language Teacher Award. Sciambi also refused to join the NEA's forced membership scheme. She too became a former teacher, as did NCBE advisory board member Carol Applegate.

In 16 states teachers are routinely fired for the only reason that they refuse to join the tyrannical NEA. And this is a union claiming to fight for teachers' rights?

What frightens the NEA is a poll in the September 1981 issue of *Instructor* magazine which showed that 82 percent of educators favor "right to work" laws. Of these 72 per-cent were union members.

Right to work laws permit teachers to work regardless of whether they join the NEA union or not. Union membership should be voluntary, for teachers who believe the NEA represents their interests. In a free country, people's arms should not be twisted, their jobs terminated, and their paychecks substantially reduced, just because they don't want to join a blatantly leftist political union.

Says Bob Sullivan, president of Professional Educators in Washington, "Teaching children is too important to allow it to be enmeshed in politics—it is essential to protect the academic freedom of all teachers and keep politics out of schools." He adds, "Forcing teachers to pay dues to any special interst group is inherently wrong and very dangerous."

As Thomas Jefferson himself wrote, "To compel a man to furnish contributions for the propagation of ideas which he disagrees with is sinful and tyrannical."

Many teachers, indeed the vast majority, disagree with the NEA's political agenda of socialism and internationalism. Yet they are in many cases being forced to hand over money to the union.

Says Frank Annunzio, Congressman from Illinois, of the NEA negative check off scheme: "It just isn't voluntary" and "It leaves a bad taste in my mouth."

When the court ordered the NEA to refund monies illegally collected through its negative check off scheme, it did not comply with the court order to do so by May 15, 1979.

As a result many teachers did not cash their checks before the August, 1979 deadline, having taken off for summer vacations. So the NEA got to keep much of its money, after all.

NEA spokesmen pretended to be sorry that not all teachers got their money back. They claimed to be "unable" to return more than $50,000 of their illegally acquired money.

The NEA has also tried to use compulsory teacher dues for left-wing political goals, which is prohibited by law. The NEA first tried to accelerate the collection of contributions to NEA-PAC, its political action committee, by treating the first of 10 installment payments of annual dues as the contribution.

The Federal Election Commission vetoed this NEA proposal, calling it an illegal contribution by the union to its own political action arm.

In another case the NEA tried to use compulsory teacher dues to pay the expenses of 451 NEA delegates to the Democratic Party convention—a blatant abridgement of FEC regulations.

When the FEC objected to this chicanery, the NEA got around the objection by having NEA-PAC pick up some of the tab for its Democratic Party delegates.

All this is intended to suggest that the NEA is bent on controlling all teachers who enter the profession, milking them for money, and then using that money for partisan ends which do not represent the views of paying teachers.

But the NEA has frankly admitted its desire to control teachers' lives. In 1970, at the NEA Annual Convention, union president George Fischer proclaimed that the union intends to control "who enters, who stays, and who leaves the profession. Once this is done we can also control the teacher training institutions."

In 1972 NEA president Catherine Barrett said, "We are the biggest potential political striking force in this country, and we are determined to control the direction of education."

In 1974 NEA president Helen Wise said, "We must seek professional standards and practices legislation in every state so that we have a meaningful voice in how teachers are trained, and who enters the profession."

Countless numbers of teachers who have resisted this NEA program to control their lives have been harassed or driven from the profession.

Earlier I quoted from the Alinksy Report for teacher organizers prepared for the NEA and used by several chapters. In that report Alinsky says, "Forget the older teachers four or five years from retirement. They will fight organizing."

Again we see that the NEA isn't concerned about even its members, only those who fall in line with its leftist agenda. The old and the conservative—they can wither away, or lose their jobs. It is the Marxists and the socialists, the militants and the radicals, the one-worlders and the secular humanists, who will find job fulfillment and advancement within the NEA.

Liberal columnist David Broder has estimated that more than 40 percent of NEA teacher members are Republicans. Yet the NEA routinely excoriates the Republican cause, denounces President Reagan, and unabashedly affiliates itself with Democratic Party officials and Democratic Party positions. This is representation?

Those who run the NEA in Washington think of it as "their organization." They know what is best for teachers. The views of teachers, especially the more traditionally minded ones, are considered to be a minor nuisance that is most safely ignored.

The NEA has a top-down structure which repudiates democracy. It is not accountable to its members. Elected NEA officials exercise little or no power. Even the current NEA president Mary Futrell, a black woman, is mostly there for token purposes. She presides over meetings but has little real power. She is, in practice, subservient to the professional staff.

Don Cameron, executive director of the NEA, and Terry Herndon, former executive director, weild most of the power.

NEA documents give the executive director, who is not

71

elected, the "primary responsibility for implementing the policies of the Association," including the power to "employ, direct, and supervise all Association staff." Who chooses the NEA director? Not the members. Nine people, meeting in closed session.

It is not surprising that teachers should be so excluded from the administrative apparatus of the NEA. The NEA was, from the start, an education organization dominated by principals and school administrators. It vehemently opposed the process of collective bargaining, and indeed in many cases favored school administrators over teachers.

But now the NEA speaks up strongly in favor of teachers' strikes. Here it forgets that education is a skilled profession, not an unskilled labor union. The NEA on the one hand wants teachers to be elevated to the rank of a doctor or a lawyer. This is a legitimate goal.

But on the other hand the NEA calls for strikes. When is the last time you saw a doctor walk out on an operation because the hospital refused a fee hike? When is the last time a lawyer picketed his office because of bad working conditions?

Who suffers when teachers strike? Not the school board, the voters or the parents. They have already got their education. It is the children, the ones the teachers are supposed to be helping, who suffer most.

It is hard to take the NEA seriously when it claims that its primary interest is the education of children and at the same time calls for teachers strikes.

Despite calls for higher wages and teachers' strikes, the NEA has lost more than 50,000 members in the last few years. An American Federation of Teachers (AFT) document explains why: "We think the NEA has been promoting views which teachers do not agree with. Many NEA policies have done serious harm to teachers, students, and our schools. We think that, rather than advancing the cause of our profession, the NEA has actually contributed to a negative public image. And rather than bolstering support for public education, NEA activities have frequently undermined it."

Take an example. The NEA Convention in 1980 adopted a resolution on the issue of nuclear power which was pretty non-partisan, at least on the surface. It called for "the efficient use of energy from all sources," the "establishment of education programs to increase public understanding of energy and alternative energy sources," and "programs that would educate the public to the dangers and benefits of nuclear power and the problems of nuclear waste disposal."

This was a proposal voted on by NEA delegates, who represent NEA members. So it was arrived at democratically, and can be considered to reasonably represent the NEA membership.

But when NEA officials got back to Washington, what did they do in terms of implementing this even-handed proposal? They gave unqualified NEA support to the "March on Harrisburg—No More Three Mile Island" protest rally against nuclear power which took place on March 28, 1981.

The NEA was mentioned on all the publicity brochures calling for a stop to this "nuclear nightmare." Inflammatory language was used throughout the petitions. And the NEA was quoted calling for an end to the use of nuclear power.

The Pennsylvania affiliate of the NEA, started to discover this anti-nuke activism on the part of the national Association, passed a resolution calling for "the NEA (to) withdraw any support for and rescind any endorsement of the planned march on Harrisburg."

Note that it is Pennsylvania teachers who asked for this; presumably Three-Mile Island threatened their own areas. But they felt the NEA was not standing up for their safety, only for its own leftist ideology.

After the Pennsylvania petition was handed to the NEA, the union's officials took the position that NEA endorsement of the Harrisburg march should not be construed to mean that the NEA has a position "for or against nuclear power."

This was sheer duplicity. It would be rather like running for election on the Democratic ticket and then claiming that people should not understand you to support the ideas of the Democratic Party.

Now the NEA frequently claims to be in favor of excellence in education. We assume this means teacher excellence. But does it?

In 1979-1980 college students planning to become teachers scored an average of 339 on the verbal portion of the SAT, more than 80 points below the national average. Math scores of these students were equally dismal.

And there is every indication that these uneducated students are going on to become uneducated teachers. Reading tests at the University of South Carolina showed that 25 percent of teachers read below the eighth grade level.

About 45 percent of the applicants for jobs as English teachers in Montgomery County, Maryland, failed an exam in the subject.

Several hundred applicants for teaching jobs in Pinellas County, Florida failed to demonstrate the required eighth-grade proficiency in basic math.

In Dallas, Texas, 262 out of 535 first year teachers failed tests in simple math and verbal ability.

Said the National Commission on Excellence, "Half of newly employed math, science, and English teachers are not qualified to teach these subjects; fewer than one third of U.S. higher schools offer physics taught by qualified teachers."

We are in nothing less than a crisis of competence. Says syndicated columnist Ralph De Toledano:

"We are in a situation where teachers are incompetent in their subject and semi-literate in the basics."

Columnist Jeffrey Hart:

"In most states you can't teach in the public schools unless you have graduated from a teachers' college. Teachers' colleges have historically emphasized not content but method. So you have people trying to teach mathematics who don't know mathematics, and you have people trying to teach English who can't speak or write English."

Not only are teachers inadequate, but in two important disciplines there is an acute shortage of them. Said the National Commission on Excellence:

"Despite widespread publicity about an overpopulation of teachers, severe shortages of certain kinds of teachers exists: in the fields of mathematics, science, and foreign languages, and among specialists in education for gifted and talented, language minority, and handicapped students.

"The shortage of teachers in mathematics and science is particularly severe."

A 1981 survey of 45 states revealed math teacher shortages in 43 states, critical shortages of earth science teachers in 33 states, and shortages of physics teachers in every single state.

The state of Minnesota reportedly trained only one physics teacher last year; in New York, out of 15,000 teaching graduates in 1981, only 61 were certified to teach chemistry.

The reason for these shortages? Simply the fact that math and science graduates earn only about $12,000 to $15,000 as teachers, while they can make $20,000 or more if they join private business, especially computer firms, which are snapping up these graduates at lucrative salaries.

Editorializes the *Washington Monthly,* the liberal magazine, about this dilemma:

"The obvious solution is to pay math and science teachers what's necessary to attract enough of them to the profession."

In other words, make education a bit more receptive to the free market. Pay teachers what they are worth in terms of the laws of supply and demand. If math and science teachers are paid more, perhaps more students would become math and science teachers, attracted by higher wages, and the shortages would not persist.

But the NEA is dead against these ideas. An NEA statement says, "NEA maintains that salary schedules should not discriminate among grade levels or subjects." Why? This "threatens teacher morale, violates the principle of equity, and depletes funds for other important educational items that teachers need in order to do their jobs."

Says the NEA, "The only acceptable answer is compensation for all teachers that will make education an attractive career. This means that educational budgets must increase substantially."

The old song: more money for education. But will this really solve the problem? It's not how it works in the private sector. There people who do jobs in demand get paid more. Computer scientists get paid more than janitors, because fewer people are qualified to be computer scientists.

Nobody in the private sector recommends paying everybody the same for the same job, and then if shortages develop in certain areas, recommends paying everybody more money so that all areas in general become more attractive to workers. No one recommends such equalitarianism, that is, except the socialists.

Why is the NEA against paying math and science teachers more? For the same reason that it is against "merit pay," the bold and innovative solution to the problem of teacher incompetence proposed by President Reagan.

Merit pay says that teachers who teach better should get paid more. Why? So that this encourages more teachers to teach better. So that excellence is subsidized and incompetence is punished.

The NEA opposes merit pay for one simple reason. Many of its own members are incompetent. They would not pass minimal tests to assure their qualification to teach. The NEA wants to protect its unqualified members. Not because it cares about their interests so much as because it wants them to remain teachers so that it can continue to collect dues from them.

Recently the NEA released a statement announcing that it "remains categorically opposed to any salary scheme based on favoritism, subjective evaluation or other arbitrary standards."

Favoritism? Who's talking about favoritism. Merit pay is not favoritism. It is just reward for outstanding effort. Is the gold medal for someone who wins the 100 meter race in the Olympics "favoritism"? Or is it the legitimate due of one who excels?

The NEA wants more money for all its teachers, probably

so that it can up dues. But consider: salaries for private school teachers are much less than those for public school teachers. Tenure is much rarer in private schools. Education degrees are not required in many cases. And teachers are happier, less teachers quit, less want to quit, and the general quality of private school education is indisputably higher than that of public school education.

Why does the NEA oppose merit pay? The *Washington Monthly* explains:

"A major obstacle to improving public education lies in the teachers' unions—specifically the NEA, which has 1.7 million members, and the AFT, with about 500,000 members.

"That teachers have formed these unions is perfectly understandable; during most of this century they have been shabbily treated, grossly underpaid, and subject often to the petty, arbitrary actions of school administrations.

"Yet as unions these organizations are dedicated to protecting *all* their members, particularly the mediocre and downright incompetent ones. As a result their allegiance ultimately lies with the bad teacher rather than the students who've been victimized by what amounts to educational malpractice."

What is the NEA solution to the teacher incompetence problem? "More money," of course. And "more teacher credentialism."

More degrees from worthless education programs which, as Jeff Hart said, don't teach what teachers have to know in order to be teachers. Rather many education programs teach socialism. That's right. They teach such things as the inefficiency of the capitalist system, and the need to explain the wonders of socialism to students.

For example several books recommended as "curriculum

guides" by the NEA charge that capitalism is "antiquated," "oppressive," and "racist," and recommend a more "equitable" distribution of property and money: in other words, socialism.

Many of these programs are not only malicious in that they repudiate successful and democratic institutions, but they are also irrelvant to teaching. Credentialism often acts as an impediment to good teaching because teachers are deterred from entering the profession for fear of having to enroll in these terrible programs.

Teachers take numerous courses in "education" which teach them socialism. But they take very few courses in what they are supposed to teach. *Education Week* reported that in a typical state 30 percent of chemistry teachers and 63 percent of physics teachers had less than 20 semester hours of college credit in their subjects. That is less than one semester and a half out of a required eight. One can become a history teacher in Maryland with only seven semester hours of American history.

In order to test teacher knowledge, some states have instituted "minimum competency" exams. Needless to say, these are opposed by the NEA. In the first year, Louisiana found that half of its aspiring teachers failed the minimum standards test. In Alabama, the same result: but the local NAACP is suing the state, backed by the NEA, arguing that the fact that blacks don't score well on these tests shows that the tests are "biased" and "racist."

Because of the credentialism the NEA supports, schools are staffed by incompetents in many cases. Firing must be done according to tenure, the NEA says. In other words if you've managed to conceal your ignorance for a longer time, you should be allowed to remain longer in public education.

Twenty years ago the teacher who stayed after school to administer to the needs of students, to provide that extra attention, would be hailed as an asset to the community. Today that teacher would be regarded as a subversive by the NEA, which might try and get him or her fired. You see, that teacher would be "union busting," i.e. disobeying contract provisions requiring that all teachers must leave school by a certain time.

This is in the interest of education?

I have detailed how the NEA is resolutely opposed to merit pay for teachers, because it does not think educational talents are comparable. It wants all teachers to be paid the same because of its "egalitarian" ideology, according to which difference implies horrible "elitism."

But the NEA opposition to merit pay is only part of its much larger opposition to testing in general. And here we begin to see how the NEA has contributed directly to the decline in standards in public education.

Recently the NEA ran full page advertisements in newspapers and magazines across the country showing a tearful, sensitive girl with whom we can all feel a rapport. "Yesterday a bright child," the caption reads. "Today, 'below average.'"

The implication is that the fact that the little girl has scored badly on her test has branded, labeled and categorized her for life as "below average." The poor dear will never be able to study again. And it's all the fault of the insidious testing system that made this inhumane thing possible.

What do teachers feel about testing? According to the NEA's own studies, 66 percent of public school teachers feel that standardized tests are "useful in diagnosing individual student learning needs."

Says Daniel Resnick of Carnegie-Mellon University, "In education as well as in private employment, the military and civil service, the use of objective tests reflects an effort to locate talent and ability regardless of its social origins. The selections of individuals to do a job on the basis of merit and ability rather than social characteristics also expresses the American commitment to opportunity."

In other words far from keeping back historically disadvantaged groups, which the NEA purports to care about, tests enable them to move forward, because they establish a criteria (merit) other than social rank or class for advancement.

The public supports testing strongly too, surveys show. A 1979 Gallup poll revealed that 81 percent of people felt that standardized tests were "very useful" or "somewhat useful" while only 17 percent rated them "not too useful." Minority parents rated tests even more highly than white parents.

What does the NEA feel about testing? According to an NEA resolution, "Intelligence, aptitude, and achievement tests have historically been used to differentiate rather than to measure performance and have, therefore, prevented equal educational opportunities for all students, particularly minorities, lower socio-economic groups, and women."

It is a most peculiar argument that because some people score lower than others on tests—test are invalid.

That is like saying that because somebody finishes first in a 100 yard dash, that means that the race is invalid and the judges are partial.

The NEA views tests as "biased," "discriminatory," and "damaging to the student's self-concept." It also rejects any test to "compare individual schools or teachers" or as "a basis for monetary renumeration or promotions."

Terry Herndon, former NEA executive director, describes standardized tests as "similar to narcotics" and compares the Educational Testing Service to "armaments manufacturers who say guns don't kill, people do."

This NEA war against testing has been inspired by Ralph Nader, who wants all tests abolished so that all men will truly be equal. Fortunately Nader and the NEA have not been successful in abolishing tests by an act of Congress, partly through the opposition to their plans by the AFT, whose president Albert Shanker says, "We believe that tests tell us things that are important for students, parents, teachers, colleges, government, and the society at large. We also believe the public unquestionably has a right to know what we are doing in the schools—how well or how badly."

Here another reason surfaces for the NEA opposition to tests. You see, tests show what a disastrous job the NEA has been doing. It reveals many NEA members to be utterly incompetent. It shows that students are not learning as much as the NEA says they have been learning.

If you are too fat to run in a race, it is understandable for you to view all races as evil and racially discriminatory. This is the situation with the NEA.

The NEA is opposed to testing students, but it is even more vociferously opposed to testing teachers. The NEA believes that it, yes the NEA, should control all teacher training and testing via an "autonomous agency" that would be "governed by a majority of teachers who are members of the majority national teachers' organization, to approve teacher preparation programs and certificate prospective teachers."

But the NEA's idea of a teacher education program is so opposed to merit, so ideological, and so comprised of jargon as differentiated from substance, that most universities would be reluctant to keep such programs in their curriculum, lest they be disgraced. The low level of intellectual challenge posed by the NEA sponsored teacher education programs is one reason so many intelligent people are staying away from the teaching profession.

In 1982 the NEA released a 64 page "Action Plan" for excellence in the schools. But it ignored the real problems facing education, in particular that of unqualified teachers and lousy teacher education programs.

As Virginia Robinson, editor of *Education Times,* observed, "Missing from the NEA position paper is any attempt to assess existing teacher education programs. It does not address one of the most troublesome problems currently plaguing teacher education—the evidently poor academic qualifications of teacher candidates. There is no mention of test scores, on which teacher candidates evidently rank well below entrants to most other professional preparations."

What is the result of having such mediocre teachers in our public schools? President Johnson of Fisk University states the obvious: "Staffing schools with mediocre teachers merely enables them to transmit their mediocrity to students."

Says Sterling M. McMurrin, former U.S. Commissioner of Education, "Larger numbers of teachers are inadequately prepared in the subject matter they teach as well as in the elements of a genuinely liberal education. This, in my view, is the major weakness of American education."

The NEA always complains that teachers are paid less than doctors, lawyers, and members of other professions, but in most if not all other professions there are rigid standards of competence that have to be met, entrance examinations that have to be passed, and severe penalties for malpractice.

If a doctor is proved incompetent he is driven from the profession. If a teacher is proved incompetent the NEA wants that teacher to be paid more.

Is it any wonder that teaching is one of the professions held in lesser regard today? Is it any wonder that, when teachers are held exempt from competence testing by the NEA, students in the U.S. were found less prepared for college and work than students from other countries, including some undeveloped countries? Perhaps the NEA will charge that those tests are invalid too.

One effective method of testing teachers, recommended by the National Council for Better Education (NCBE), is the one used in some California schools. There teachers are given a set of objective questions and answers and placed in a class of students unfamiliar to them.

The teacher has been given time to study the questions and answers beforehand, but the kids have not. The challenge before the teacher is to convey or teach this information to students.

Later the kids are tested to see how well they learned. And their grade is also the teacher's grade. Because how well they learn is, in large measure, a reflection of how well the teacher teaches.

The problem with the NEA opposing tests for teachers is, in part, that this resistance to testing passes along to students. Says the distinguished journalist Vermont Royster, "The root of the problem of modern education is the idea that young people shouldn't be required to learn anything and be accountable for it. The prevailing doctrine has long been that if a young person is put in the requisite number of years in school, he was entitled to a diploma."

Where do the kids get this idea? From their teachers, of course.

And from the NEA, whose booklet "Testing—It's Uses and Abuses" calls for "a world without tests" so that we can "constantly revise our notions of a person's skills and performance." This would enable us to "adjust our thinking to live comfortably in a no test world," the NEA says. Other stated objections to evaluative tests cited in the booklet, quoted verbatim:

—Tests don't help teachers teach. In fact they are often obstacles to good teaching.

—They do not enable teachers to diagnose students' learning problems.

—They do not help teachers prescribe remedies for students' learning problems.

—They take inordinate amounts of time to prepare for, administer, and score.

—They are often constructed so that the questions are too ambiguous to be answered with a single word or phrase.

—They often contain inaccurate information based on incorrect sources.

Now some of this is pure nonsense. Tests do not "often" contain inaccurate information; that is why when an SAT or other standardized test has a single error (out of several hundred questions) it makes newspaper articles.

Other stated objections are simply irrelevant. Perhaps tests do not by themselves diagnose why students learn slowly, or propose remedies. But neither do tests tell why Dewey lost the election to Truman. The point is: tests serve admittedly limited objectives, but serve them well.

The point to remember about testing is that there is a difference between standards and arbitrary privilege. Tests are not elitist because they refute the possibility that everyone is right. The fact that some groups score less than other groups does not, by itself, prove heinous racism. In fact tests are a pretty objective measure of talent, and it is talent which does not take into account social standing or race. Thus testing works against other criteria of advancement.

We are working toward a fair society, an "equal opportunity" society, in which hopefully men will be judged by their performance and not because of other characteristics such as class or skin color.

But does the NEA want this? Not if their brochures are to be believed.

The NEA itself does not believe in equal opportunity for the races. The union has endorsed an outright quota system which it carries to ridiculous lengths.

Says the NEA bylaws, "It is the policy of the Association to achieve ethnic-minority delegate representation at least equal to the proportion of identified ethnic-minority populations within each state."

Any state NEA affiliate which fails to achieve "total state and local delegation which reflects these ethnic-minority populations risks being denied the right to participate in the annual convention."

The NEA Constitution requires that "members from ethnic minorities shall comprise at least 20 percent of the board." This quota will be met even if it is necessary to elect additional directors "to assure such minority representation." States must similarly meet these quotas; if the first three directors from a state don't include a minority, a fourth director should be chosen "who is from an ethnic-minority group."

This is almost a caricature of affirmative action. Perhaps most absurd is the way the NEA identifies "human and civil rights awards" at its annual convention, and identifies the race of the recipient in its programs and during the introductory speeches.

How would you like to see your name appear in a program thus:

Jack Rosenthal, Civil Rights Award, Jew.

Or Mike Johnson, Human Rights Award, Black.

The NEA was charged with having an unconstitutional quota system that discriminated against whites. Now it simply calls its quotas "goals" but continues to implement them with the same rigor.

In the Washington office of the NEA there is a Committee on Minority Affairs "composed of four representatives of each of the following groups: American Indian or Alaskan native, Asian, Black, and Chicano-Hispanic." These "ethnic subcommittees" are supposed to make sure that "goals" for minority representation are fulfilled and to "provide minority input on NEA programs and policies."

Under section four of the NEA constitution we find the following clause:

"If after eleven years no member of an ethnic-minority group has served as President, nomination at the subsequent Representative Assembly shall be restricted to members of such groups."

No wonder that the current NEA President Mary Futrell is a black woman. Now the NEA can feel safe until at least 1995.

The NEA places its emphasis on minority quotas even higher than it stresses seniority. A contract the NEA negotiated in South Bend, Indiana, said clearly that "no minority bargaining unit member shall be laid off." Period.

There is even an NEA Committee on Women's Concerns, which is a bit much since women are no minority in the NEA: in fact they comprise more than 75 percent of the membership.

Not only does the NEA support quotas for women and blacks, but also for homosexuals. This is specified in NEA Resolution E-5 which calls for reverse discrimination based on "sexual orientation."

The rest of society is considering the question of whether it is wise for homosexuals to teach at all in public schools, whether their lifestyle makes an impact on their teaching style and on students. And here the NEA is telling us that we should give *preference* to homosexuals.

Late in 1981 the NEA helped prepare a booklet on the Ku Klux Klan and the struggle for equality which was intended for classroom use.

The Anti-Defamation League of B'nai Brith denounced the booklet as "anti-American propaganda" because it portrays this country as "inherently racist."

Albert Shanker, president of the AFT, said, "It asks teachers to tell their students that practically no progress has been made by blacks."

The NEA booklet concludes, "It is important to remember that the Klan is only the tip of the iceberg, the most visible and obvious manifestation of the entrenched racism in our society."

The NEA's love for racial radicalism apparently extends to the Third World sphere. At the July 1982 NEA Convention delegates were given a book. One section, titled, "What is Miseducation of Third World People?" contained the allegation that Third World students were being misled by having their intelligence measured by culturally biased tests.

Another, more egregious, section of the book asked "What I as an educator must know in order to deal effectively with negating the miseducation of Third World Students."

Among these pedagogic "musts" were the following:

—"Acknowledge that the society in the United States is racist. Since the educational system is only a microcosm of the society, it is racist too."

—"Admit that the educational system in the United States was not established to produce Third World people who are politically and economically salient (sic) and who also maintain a Third World consciousness."

—"Acknowledge that power concedes to nothing other than power superior to itself. (Remember, when you confront the system, the system will *deal* with you.)"

Similar sentiments are expressed in the NEA volume *Cross-cultural Education* which it distributes as part of its curriculum library.

Here is how the NEA suggests a class dealing with the OPEC oil embargo be taught:

"The economics class might address the nomenclature of the international economic system, exploring how it is possible that a few Western nations control the flow of goods and services around the world. A mode of enquiry might center around the statement that three million whites in Africa enjoy a very high standard of living, while 15 million blacks on the same continent exist essentially in economic slavery. The language arts class might explore the reasons why English is the international language or examine the influence of English in promulgating European values and attitudes among non-European nations. The political science class might explore the sociopolitical impact of the oil embargo on American multinational corporations operating in newly decolonized countries such as Angola and Mozambique."

All this is cited not just to show the NEA's warped and racist attitudes, but also to suggest that the NEA is working overtime to pass these damaging ideas to your children in the classroom. After all these are not private opinions that simply happen to be held by NEA bosses, and happen to be embodied in the NEA's own structure; these are ideas that the NEA is openly and actively employing in textbooks; these are ideas that the NEA is drilling into the heads of teachers; these are ideas the NEA is imposing on public education in general.

Take another example. The NEA, in a joint venture with the Council on Interracial Books for Children, put out a 1981 report on romantic novels.

It did not criticize the novels for their sentimental, unrealistic view of life. It did not impugn them for being badly written. It did not suggest that there are better things for children to be reading.

Instead the NEA launched a campaign to "eliminate bias" from children's books. What kind of bias? Well, bias toward heterosexual love, for instance.

In one of the articles in the report, a self-described "adult lesbian" observes, "No romantic novel ever gave me the slightest hint that women and girls could, and did, stay together."

She added, "Fortunately, I eventually escaped from the entrapment of these novels. I am concerned that the adolescent years of those who may be gay or lesbian and are now reading these happiness package novels will be made far more difficult than necessary."

And what about the heterosexual students who may be damaged by reading stories of homosexual affairs? Sodomy does not exactly have a salubrious effect on the adolescent mind.

Whether you are a parent or teacher, you know as well as I do that children are very impressionable. Science has proved that many of their ideas and values are developed not in adolescence or middle age but indeed in very early life.

We entrust our teachers with the task of taking care of our children, with imbuing in them the right values: dignity, courage, sacrifice, love, character, honor, integrity. These values are an extention of the parent and the home.

Instead we find that the NEA is pushing teachers in a different direction. It wants our children to be tutored in affection to the Soviet Union, hatred for America and the American way of life. It wants our children to reject the democratic and free enterprise systems (without even really understanding them) and take up socialism and Communism instead. It wants our children to, far from abandoning ideas of placing one race above another, actively and conscious-ly discriminate against whites and in favor of minorities. It wants our kids to develop anti-Western and anti-business ideas and to cultivate militant Third World sensibilities.

Socrates was put to death for less. If you remember, he was tried for the crime of corrupting the children. It turned out that Socrates was innocent. And I don't mean to com-pare the good philosopher to the NEA, most of whose officials are semi-literature ideologues, who insult the mem-ory of Socrates.

But the NEA is guilty of the crime of which Socrates was accused, and while it is too much to recommend criminal penalties for NEA officials like Cameron and Herndon, it is not too much to recommend the death penalty for the NEA and its cabinet arm, the Department of Education. These are two organizations which have betrayed teach-ers, and virtually ruined public education in America.

It is a fact well known to all educators and most of the American public that private schools far outperform public schools in this country.

They provide better education, both in terms of the liberal arts as well as vocational training, better discipline and transmission of morals values, and at a lower cost.

This has been extensively documented in studies such as the Coleman Report. But perhaps the best measure of it is the fact that some of the most strident advocates of the public schools nevertheless send their own kids to private school.

Take Jesse Jackson. For the last several years, bankrolled by $3 million in federal money, Jackson has been singing the praises of the public schools. But as a parent he takes no chances. His own son is sent to St Albans, an exclusive private school in Washington D.C. Other politicians do the same as Jackson.

Take another case. In 1960 Ruby Bridges endured the catcalls and violent epithets of white racists to become the first black to enroll in New Orleans' segregated school system. This was regarded as a heroic victory for integrated public education. But recently Bridges, now 28 and married, took all her three children *out* of the New Orleans public school system to enroll them in a parochial Christian school. She explains, "I don't like to put down public schools, but my children really weren't learning the way they should have."

Recently the *Washington Monthly* described a top NEA official who denounced the present administration for "trying to destroy public education" with their proposal for tuition tax credits. "He too sends his son to private school," the liberal magazine observed wrily.

Reagan's tax credit proposal is well intentioned. It seeks to rectify a built-in inequity in the education system. Parents who send their kids to private school must pay twice for education: once in the form of taxes which support the public schools, and again in the form of private school tuition and costs. This is unfair. Hence a tax credit.

I support the idea of tax credits, but not at the federal level. I would much rather leave educational decisions to states and communities. If states want to give their residents the privilege of choosing between public and private education through the means of a tax credit, I'm for that. If they don't, that's up to them.

One reason I think local communities would do well to adopt tax credits, in my opinion, is that they would generate *competition* between private and public education. This cannot but be healthy. I believe one of the reasons public education is so bad is because it is monopolistic. That has made it susceptible not to the pressures of educational needs or parents, but to the outside pressures of the NEA and other radical groups which work neither in the interest of parents nor of education.

Needless to say, the NEA opposes tax credits. It complains that money would go to "mostly church related institutions," revealing a bit of its anti-religious bias. But most importantly the NEA wants to retain its strangle-hold on American education. It detests the free market both on principle (it contrasts with the NEA's own socialist leaning objectives) and in practice (it takes away from the NEA's power).

Yet the NEA couches its opposition to tax credits in different terms. Speaking before an NEA conference Charles Park, a University of Wisconsin professor, said the tax credit proposal was advanced by "supporters of the new evangelical far right" and epitomized the "current attacks on the public schools."

This sort of inflammatory rhetoric misses the point and does little by way of constructive analysis of Reagan's tax credit proposal or anything else. Other wild charges flit about the offices of the NEA, among them the claim that private schools don't admit many blacks.

But research has proved this completely false. In fact it is minorities, in greater numbers than ever, who are pulling their children out of the public schools. Catholic schools enroll large percentages of minority children. A recent survey by the Catholic League for Religious and Civil Rights also put to rest the theory that private schools were only for the rich: the survey showed that 72 percent of private school parents earn less than $15,000 per year.

This means that parents are, at great personal and family sacrifice, sending their children to private schools. They prefer private schools, despite their expense, to free public schools. This says a great deal about the ruin of public education today.

This ruin the NEA wants to preserve. It has sent out several questionnaires to Congressmen. "NEA has always been opposed to any legislation designed to provide tax credits for tuition paid to any institution. We see such a scheme unsound financially as well as constitutionally."

This, of course, confuses the financial interests of the

NEA with those of poor and middle class parents. And it assumes that what furthers the power of the NEA is automatically what is mandated by the U.S. Constitution.

The NEA questionnaire goes on:

"Assuming your victory in the forthcoming election, what role would you envision for the teachers in your District and our NEA representatives in Washington with regard to your duties as a Member of Congress?"

The tone of that question betrays the NEA's monopolistic goals for public (and private) education in America. Says columnist William Murchison, "Nothing short of total control of the young generation's mental and moral development will satisfy the NEA."

The NEA hates locally controlled programs, even in public education, because diversity works against its goal of centralized control. "The multiplicity of existing programs, many of which have conflicting or duplicative purposes," says an NEA brochure, "confuses local educators and does not provide a means for adequate planning and development of a balanced educational program at the local level."

The NEA has had its claws into Walter Mondale for some time now, and since 1976 Mondale has sponsored the NEA's bid for monopoly control in the Senate and in public life.

In 1976, senators Alan Cranston, and Walter Mondale sponsored a bill which now appears as part of the Education Amendments of 1976. This bill was largely *written* by the NEA. It calls for a three year federal grant of $203 million for "teachers centers" that would work on teacher training and curriculum development. The catch: Each center would be run by a "policy board" made up of the majority of teachers in the area. Federal regulations allow for the appointment of these teachers by the union—this means NEA control of the policy board. The *Reader's Digest* wondered of this bill, "Neither Senate nor House seems to have held a single hearing to find out whether such centers actually need federal financing, or why Washington should try to induce elected school boards to turn over their own statutory duties to non-elected union officials."

Another blow to the head of parent's rights. Whooped the NEA joyfully after the Mondale-Cranston bill was passed: "For the first time federal law has cut teachers into policy making."

What does this drive for total control lead to? Inefficiency and totalitarianism.

Since the NEA established its grip on public education, the bureaucracy has ballooned. Mountains of paperwork have resulted from NEA sponsored bills which have become law. These regulations force schools to hire fewer teachers and more administrators to fill out more government forms. Valuable attention is taken away from the classroom and focused on Washington. The mode of thinking becomes not: how can we better educate children? Instead: how can we get another federal grant?

Recently the Department of Education funded new computer course-ware in math, elementary reading, writing, and science. The NEA produced a "Yellow Book" directory of educational software, including more than 100 programs which have been "teacher certified" by the NEA. Computer companies are charged more than $1000 to have their products evaluated; a source of convenient revenue to the NEA. And all for the privilege of getting the imprimatur of this powerful and reckless lobby.

The fact that the NEA prepares and profits from these software evaluations, and the fact that it uses its role as the teachers' representative to foist these goods on the teachers of the nation, pose series questions of conflict of interest. But it has never entered the NEA's head that it might be acting out of corruption. "What's good for the NEA is good for America," seems to be the governing motif of arrogant NEA officials in Washington.

First corruption, then totalitarianism. Often the latter comes into being to protect the interests of a decaying bureaucracy which is being threatened by private, more efficient alternatives.

In a 1980 study in the *NEA Review* the union approvingly quoted Edward Morgan saying this: "It isn't that the New Right should be crushed, its somber voice silenced. This is a free country, still, and they have a right to express their beliefs. They do *not* have the right, however, in an open society, to believe as they believe, to do as they do, to behave as they behave."

This leads to the following reflection from journalist Allan Stang, "I have read this masterpiece a dozen times, hoping all along that I have been misreading, and that it doesn't say what it says. But it does. According to NEA via Morgan, you have the right to express your beliefs, but not to believe them. How that is possible, I don't know." Stang wrily speculates that perhaps "Morgan was sniffing something he shouldn't when he wrote it."

Less funny is the attitude the NEA takes toward the issue of discipline in schools. In a sense we have an irony here: the NEA, which supports strong-arm governments around the world (as long as they are far-leftist or Communist), which wants to exert a steel grip on education, nevertheless professes to deplore discipline and strength as a means to arrive at desirable goals.

Now it turns out that most Americans believe that

98

totalitarianism is bad, because it stifles rights and kills people, but a little school discipline is good, because it inculcates in children values and ideas that enhance and defend this great and free society. But the NEA believes the opposite.

Not only is the idea of discipline anathema to the NEA, but in some cases the union positively *encourages* lawless and hooliganish behavior, imploying that these traits accompany moral passion. This is especially the case when blacks commit crimes: they are simply expressing distaste for a society which has kept them down, in the analysis of the NEA.

When Senator Birch Bayh held Senate Judiciary Committee hearings on violence and vandalism in schools, the then-president of the NEA testified that youth alienation came from "hostilities in South East Asia" and "Watergate." The real cause of violence in our schools, the NEA spokesman said, was "the country's reliance on military force" and "the increased use of violence in the society."

I have never met a student who cut classes and broke things because of Watergate; maybe you have. But the point is: the NEA is seeking to exempt delinquents and criminals of all responsibility for their actions. Schools who attempt to discipline students are guilty of "outmoded disiplinary and educational practices." They are "institutionally inflexible in meeting individual student needs."

An NEA review of textbooks included a study of a Harper and Row children's novel about a 14 year old Puerto Rican "street punk" who steals and whose father beats people. The study praised the kid for being a "hustler with morals"—he had "hustled a full meal from a sympathetic waitress but left her a large tip, explaining, 'I'm broke for restaurants, not people.' " This is the NEA's idea of high morality.

More astonishing, the NEA asks readers to admire the kid's father, who is "in Attica for having assaulted a policeman during a Puerto Rican independence day rally" which "suggests that he has a sense of self-respect and self-determination."

No wonder that we find statements in the NEA's brochure on "Discipline: How Parents Can Help" like the following:

"Punishment and reward belong in an autocratic social system. With the greater realization of democracy as a way of life, parents can no longer assume the role of autocratic authority. Today our whole social structure has changed. Our power over young people is sharply diminished, and they know it whether we do or not."

But it is one thing to say that discipline is not an effective way to control young people—this is a false but acceptable statement—but quite another to say that indiscipline, vandalism, and violence are desirable expressions of social maturity on the parts of children and their elders.

The NEA's tactic in fighting discipline in schools is always to focus on a tiny minority of cases where excessive discipline has been used, and to imply that these cases are representative of most parents and most children.

For example, in a similar case, the NEA has reasoned from the fact that some children get marijuana even though it is illegal, to the conclusion that it is desirable to legalize marijuana because anybody who wants it can easily get it.

Not true. Laws serve as moral statements. Some things are illegal even though they cannot be effectively enforced, because they make an assertion about how society views certain actions.

What is the result of the NEA's crusade against discipline? NEA's own surveys catalog it: in 1979 the NEA itself reported 120,000 physical attacks on teachers by students.

The reason for this is that parental discipline of children has been interpreted as necessarily being "authoritarian" or "child abuse" and teacher's discipline has been viewed as "vicious" and "unconstitutional." The NEA wants, instead, such weird and leftist characters as pseudo-psychologists, group therapists, untrained "facilitators" and assorted radicals and groupies to "interact" with your children and show them the high road to Gandhian nirvana and non-violence.

The kids react to this by beating up the psychologists and therapists and vandalizing the schools. More psychologists and therapists are called in to "understand" what the students have done, and to help them "identify the hostile feelings" in themselves which have led them to this.

It's a mess, as you can see. What is particularly sad about the indiscipline that pervades our public school system is not just the extreme cases—the vandalizers and hooligans—but also the average student who is affected by the chaos and disorder. Charles Silberman writes in *Crisis in the Classroom:*

"Adults fail to appreciate what grim, joyless places most American schools are, how petty are the rules by which they are governed, how intellectually sterile and barren the atmosphere, what an appalling lack of civility obtains."

Children don't feel good when they are pandered to by unenthusiastic people without any sense of discipline and order; they feel good about themselves when they operate under certain rules, certain restraints. They feel good about themselves when they accomplish something, when they learn something, when they acquire skills and participate with others in serious, structured activity.

An article in *Today's Education* (May 1983) outlines another problem:

"The assumption of the education professors was that when a lower economic class black student enters school his main problems are psychological and societal—perhaps a defeatist attitude coupled with an uncaring and still partly racist environment—rather than more devastating shortcomings that have nothing to do with race: great ignorance of facts, and of how to reason, very poor work and study habits, or poorly formed character."

The result? "We are understandably loath to admit we are bringing up large numbers of children to be truly stupid, permanently so after a certain age, and worse, bringing up some to have characters so poor they are incapable of living lives useful to themselves or society."

One solution: "What is needed, within the limits of what the schools can provide, is very simple: Tough, demanding teachers and school officials, with authority to put pressure on students, and who will kick kids' behinds, metaphorically speaking, until they do their homework, do lots of it, do it accurately, do it on time, do it in correct English, and take criticism with civility."

What a far cry from what the NEA is proposing and working toward.

The problem of discipline is best seen in the context of the larger problem of moral license. Briefly, the NEA does not believe that traditional morals have a place in public education. Its documents imply that any attempt to teach kids traditional morals fails to take into account that this is a modern society and also that there is a prohibition against mixing church and state.

But the NEA fails to understand that morals are an intrinsic part of education. As educator John Howard puts it, "Excellence without a context has no meaning. Fagin was an excellent teacher of pickpockets." The NEA still failed to see the moral chaos it was perpetrating.

All the signs were there: students were copulating in school. Illegal marijuana was available. Alcohol was consumed in dangerous quantities. Foul language was pervasive.

Not only did the NEA close its eye to all this, but it implicitly encouraged it. NEA members resisted all efforts to impose discipline and morality on students. "You can't legislate morality" was the slogan used, although in fact all laws are impositions of morality, and many many laws are effective. It is simply not true that students sternly penalized for consuming drugs or alcohol will continue to do so in the same amount; indeed the empirical evidence indicates that the opposite is true. Discipline works.

It is not that discipline is always needed. The reason for discipline in the school is not to impose tyrannies on students, but to cultivate in them good and decent *habits,* so that pretty soon discipline is no longer necessary to make them live their lives responsibly. Rather, our children will have learned to make it on their own. They will truly become adults.

The "values clarification" that the NEA has endorsed is, in fact, a repudiation of not only traditional morality, but all morality. That is because, as philosopher Allan Bloom says, "Value-free teaching of values is a rather self-defeating enterprise, which trivializes values by reducing them to personal preferences."

In other words, to say that "to each his own set of values" is to say that it is not important what values our children live by, which is to say values are irrelevant in society's march towards progress.

My own view is not absolute: I do not think a monolithic set of values should be imposed on children. Rather, I believe that it is the values of the parents which should be inculcated in children. It turns out that most American people hold a pretty decent set of values; I have faith in the morality and decency of the people.

But the NEA does not. It is imposing its *own* set of values on children in the name of values-clarification or value-neutrality.

How is it doing this? Consider several examples. In Spring of 1981 the NEA sent out a collection of materials deploring American support for the Duarte government in El Salvador. Former NEA head Braulio Alonso argued that Salvadoran citizens were being harmed by right-wing squads and that their union, ANDES, was being suppressed.

But the "educational" materials presented as an objective analysis of the Central American conflict by the NEA were, in fact, a severe distortion of what was occuring in Central America. Little mention was made of the Marxist government in neighbouring Nicaragua which funds the Salvadoran rebels. No mention was made of the tyrannies the Nicaraguan government imposes on its people; this is certainly relevant, because a Nicaragua-style Marxism is what the El Salvador guerillas want.

The NEA material on El Salvador was prepared with the assistance of the Committee In Solidarity With the People of El Salvador (CISPES), a pro-Marxist group. Journalist Penn Kemble says that CISPES "supports and openly campaigns for the guerilla movement" which is fighting to oust the elected government of El Salvador. CISPES is also "a mere auxiliary to the Marxist-Leninist command structure of the guerilla army," according to Kemble.

It is interesting that the NEA is so indignant about human rights violations in the democratic El Salvador government while being blind to much more egregious violations by the Nicaraguan government, or the inherent denial of rights in the Marxist-Leninist ideology.

In June 1982 the NEA weekly newsletter identified thirty "peace resource groups" to which it referred teachers. The purpose was clear: the NEA wanted teachers to get materials from these groups and teach them in the classroom to "educate" children about defense issues.

Educators for Social Responsibility was one of the groups identified by the NEA. It has published a 209 page curriculum guide for "dealing with issues of nuclear war in the classroom." In fact the guide reads like an anti-nuclear tirade. It is certainly not an objective presentation of the arguments for and against disarmament. It encourages teachers, rather, to "use imaginative literature to acquaint students with the dangers we face in our nuclear world."

In other words, show scary pictures so that kids will be frightened, and rather than be able to think clearly about nuclear issues, they will be driven by emotion into the "peace" camp.

The NEA-sponsored literature asks the question, "But who are the Soviets?" The answer: "The short story, 'The Fate of man,' by Mikhail Sholokhov, is a good choice. It is the story of a Soviet soldier in World War II; he spends time in Nazi prison camps, and returns home to find his family has been killed in a bombing attack. The World War II setting—when the U.S. and the Soviet Union were allies fighting a common enemy—may help your students bypass cold-war distortion to reach an understanding of the Soviets as people."

In other words, teachers are to be silent about gross Soviet abuses—brutal repression of Christians, Jews, dissidents, mentally ill—and focus on "niceties" about the Soviet Union. Soviet people are people too: this is the message.

Admittedly Soviet people are people, but they are not the ones in control of the Soviet government. And the Soviet government is the collective equivalent of your neighborhood butcher. This is no "cold war rhetoric," rather it is simply an historical fact. Thirty million Russians killed by Stalin is not "cold war propaganda," it is a statistic upon which no historians disagree.

We are asked by the NEA to remember the US Soviet alliance in World War II, but not to remember the preceding Soviet-Nazi alliance, which the Soviets opportunistically entered into, and abided by, until the Germans attacked Russia.

Another NEA section explains to kids about "Inflammatory Words Can Teach You to Hate." Students are asked to study the memoirs of Lt. William Calley to see how his simplistic grasp of the inflammatory word "Communism" led to his killing at MyLai. "In all my years in the army," Calley is quoted saying, "I was never taught the Communists are human beings. We weren't in Mylai to kill human beings. We were there to kill ideology."

That's all we get about Communism. It's a misunderstood term, epitomized by the naivete of Calley. All criticism of Communism is refuted by Calley's misunderstanding of it, or his exaggeration of the effect it has on people.

The values the NEA imposes on children are not restricted to the view, a moral (or more accurately immoral) view, that Communism is benign, U.S. defense policy is based on the myth of the evil of Communism, and disarmament is the solution. Indeed the NEA wants to wreck America's capacity to defend itself, so that in weakness the U.S. will submit to the Soviet Union, or better, a world form of government.

Needless to add, free enterprise would not exist in this world government. No, people's property would be forcibly taken from them and given to the unproductive members of our society. Egalitarianism, you see.

In the next chapter I examine NEA sponsorship of views to fulfill these purposes.

CHAPTER

8

The NEA endorses the liberal Council on Interracial Books which has put out plenty of material for students on international issues. One bulletin is devoted to "Militarism in Education." The subtitle: "Racism, Sexism, and Militarism: the links."

If you didn't think America's defense establishment existed to oppress blacks and women, be alerted. This is the insight the NEA wants your children to be left with.

The NEA brochures say that "militarism" is an "elitist, hierarchical ideology which values strength over human qualities and denies the equal worth of nations and individuals."

Here is how it answers "questions frequently raised about the arms race."

Q: But aren't we risking our way of life if we allow the Russians to get ahead?

A: The $1 trillion defense budget that the President seeks for the next four years will do more to undermine our democratic values and standard of living than anything the Russians can do.

Q: But how can we trust the Russians? How can we be sure they won't cheat?

A: We can trust them as much as they can trust us.

Here the NEA is spreading the gospel of unilaterial disarmament. It is in complete ignorance of the Russian history of violating arms control treaties, such as the chemical weapons ban and treaties about nuclear testing. Indeed, because Russia is a closed society, we don't even *know* how many treaties have been violated; much is made of the U.S. satellite surveillance system, but if we don't know whether Israel or South Africa (our allies, open societies, with a free press) have or don't have nuclear weapons, we cannot be confident in our ability to gauge Soviet nuclear testing.

Also the NEA advances the curious and radical notion that building up one's defenses undermines one's security. This argument simply runs counter to nature. Never in the history of the world has weakness proved an effective rebuttal to might. Indeed the opposite is true.

Do we want this kind of indoctrination for our children? Don't they have the right to be fully informed about the nature of the Soviet Union? Don't they have the right to choose what views they will hold about U.S. defense policy without having the NEA ram its theology down their throats?

It is not surprising that the NEA does not find the Soviet Union a threat, because it wants to impose Soviet-style totalitarianism on our children. In fact that is what it is doing now.

Indoctrination is always bad, because it reduces the freedom of the mind, but it is particularly insidious when applied to children, because the minds of children are not fully formed yet. To indoctrinate the minds of children is to destroy their minds, to render them unable to think and make decisions, even in the future.

An example of the NEA's forced indoctrination is "Choices: A Unit in Conflict and Nuclear War," which was funded jointly by the Union of Concerned Scientists, a radical left-wing organization, the NEA, and the Massachusetts Teachers' Organization. This booklet was made available to teachers of the 7th and 8th grade throughout the country.

In this 144 page booklet, which has 10 lessons on the danger of nuclear war, we discover that nuclear weapons are themselves evil, especially when used to defend the United States. Russian nuclear weapons, though bad, are not as evil as those of the US, because the Russians don't harbor hostile intent.

"Choices" says that the action-reaction cycle of the arms race is what threatens peace most, and the only solution is a "nuclear freeze" or unilaterial disarmament. The U.S. is seen as the instigator of every nuclear escalation, and the Soviet Union as a society compelled to respond to the villainous U.S. build-up.

In order to scare students, the NEA provides them with extremely frightening accounts of what a nuclear war would be like if it happened over their heads. Vivid descriptions of mutilated bodies are used to argue, not by logic but by emotion, that what amounts to surrender to the Soviet Union is the only way to stay alive.

"Better Red than Dead," seems to be the message of "Choices." But it fails to show that under current US policy peace is being preserved, we can be neither red nor dead, and even if we surrendered to the Russians on NEA instructions, there is no guarantee that we would not be red *and* dead.

Albert Shanker, president of the AFT, says, "Teachers have a special responsibility to be balanced and fair."

But fairness is not what we get from the NEA when it suggests that the reason for the Soviet invasion of Poland and Afghanistan was "some unfriendly countries," as though the Poles and the Afghans were to be blamed for their hostility which provoked a Soviet invasion.

Similarly the NEA argues, speciously, that it is the U.S. effort to defend itself against existing Soviet terrorism which provokes the Soviet Union into committing more barbarism. The NEA believes that if the US were not to resist the Soviets, they would be less, not more, totalitarian.

Even the *Washington Post,* which has a liberal editorial policy (and indeed news policy), criticized the NEA for "Choices," which it called "propaganda."

"This is not teaching in any normally accepted, or for that matter acceptable, sense. It is political indoctrination," the *Post* said.

Phyllis Schlafly, the women's rights leader, says that "Choices" is "a misuse of classroom responsibility by the NEA which is drilling impressionable students with left wing dogma."

The NEA was actively involved in a 1982 Solidarity Day "Peace Demonstration" in New York City. Evidence now shows that the Communist Party was actively involved in organizing and participating in the demonstration, although the news media, which has never feared Communists, presented the occasion as a "rainbow coalition" of peace activists from all walks of life.

Here is Rap Lewis writing in the official magazine of the U.S. Communist Party: "Solidarity Day gave the lie to the most commonly expressed alibi of right-wing union leaders —that the rank and file would not respond to militant initiatives. As a result, the prestige of labor has grown and the influence of the right has declined."

This Communist rhetoric is written in code, so we must decipher it. "Labor" refers to "committed communists." The "right" refers to those who oppose Soviet foreign policy.

"Peace" refers to what the U.S. arms build-up threatens, while the Soviet build-up is said to further peace. "Militant objectives" is a common euphemism used by Communists for "violent revolution."

Here is Gus Hall on the Solidarity Day demonstration. (Hall is the presidential candidate for the Communist Party, U.S.A.):

"Our Party's indispensable and unique contribution in the struggle for peace and detente must be the exposure of the Big Lie. We must work more diligently, effectively and creatively in a planned way to break through the barriers of lies, distortions, myths and supression.

"My personal experience on radio, TV, and college campuses is that once we reach people with the truth about the Soviet peace policies they respond favorably."

The *truth* about Soviet peace policies? Here we see the unequivocal pro-Soviet bent of what is being said. It is not the arms build-up per se that is being opposed, but the U.S. arms build-up.

In his article Communist Hall said, "We must assist in the organization, and where necessary the revitalization of local coalitions" in the spirit of the Solidarity Day demonstration.

In view of this, isn't it interesting that among those marching in front of the so-called "peace coalition" on Solidarity Day was Mary Futrell, current president of the NEA.

Other leftists were present: Donna Brazile, of the U.S. Student Association; Dorothy Height, president of the National Council of Negro Women; Randall Forsberg, founder of the Nuclear Freeze campaign; and Jesse Jackson, presidential candidate who wants to severely cut defense expenditures.

Arnold Becchetti, organization secretary of the U.S.

Communist Party, writes that, "We can take pride in the role of our Party and our class in the unfolding of the labor-led march on Washington of September 19, 1981, where over half a million people turned out in a great fightback demonstration.

"Our class and our party were also an *important factor* in the one-million strong peace demonstration of June 12, 1982, which raised to a new high opposition to the warlike policies of the Reagan administration."

And the media denies that the peace demonstations had any Communists.

Just how sympathetic the NEA is to Communism is clearly delineated in a line by a Communist *Daily World* reporter who wrote of the NEA's 1981 convention:

"Nowhere in the basic documents of NEA, in their resolutions or new business items, are there *any* anti-Soviet or anti-socialist positions."

What a staggering admission. The NEA is a completely pro-Soviet and pro-socialist group. If only NEA members knew this! If only the American public knew!

As an example of the NEA's hostility to the free enterprise system, consider the presence of top NEA officials at several meetings and caucuses of Socialist groups, such as the Socialist Caucus at the Democratic Party convention in 1980.

The Socialist Caucus was attended by some 250 people who passed a resolution that pledged "to move the Democratic Party beyond the limits of Keynesianism toward an economy that meets social needs through public control." As a preliminary to the Socialist Caucus meeting, a convention rally was held at New York's Town Hall; speakers included Caesar Chavez, union boss Douglas Fraser, feminist leader Eleanor Smeal, and the NEA's executive director Terry Herndon.

In early 1977 an NEA document called "A Working Economy for Americans" was made public by an NEA member who became frustrated with the NEA's leftist agenda. The NEA publication shows an intense dislike for freedom in the marketplace, economic incentive, and jobs created as a result of "capitalism."

Russell Kirk, the famous educator and author, says of the NEA publication, "It repeats like incantations many of the shallow slogans of the New Left." There is plenty of praise here for centralization, elaborate regulation, higher federal taxation, fantastically increased expenditures, and more money and more power to the Educational lobby, the NEA.

The NEA has always wanted more money, but at least in the past it proposed to use it well. Now it even discards such pretenses. It argues, rather, in the form of threat: if the public does not come up with enough ransom to pay the NEA, then public education will suffer, and the public, not the NEA, will be to blame.

The NEA will entertain no questions about why money, and only money, seems to be its always proposed solution. Psychologist Barbara Lerner pointed out in a recent article in *The Public Interest* that the U.S. already spends twice as much as the Japanese (of whose industrial superiority we make much).

So if Tokyo can do it with half the money, why can't we?

Another indicator that more money is not the solution is the fact that public schools now employ 177,000 *more* teachers than in 1969-70, for 2.7 million *fewer* pupils, and the quality of education provided to those pupils has *declined*.

For years the NEA made the argument, "More kids cost

less money." But now they can't bring themselves to ask, "Why don't fewer kids cost less money?"

Robert Poole, the editor of *Reason* magazine, tells us what the real problem is. "The fundamental reason for the failure of the public schools is their monopoly status. Today's public school system has no real competition, and hence there is no consumer soverignty. In functional terms, it exists not to turn out educated children but to provide secure jobs for teachers and administrators. It has become the very model of a self-serving, self-perpetuating bureaucracy—thanks to automatic funding from taxes, regardless of results."

Poole refutes the "more money" clamor thus: "It need not cost a penny more to require homework, discipline, performance testing, and academic rigor. Even paying more to attract math and science teachers (who are more in demand) could be accomplished by not giving raises in other fields and utilizing savings from declining enrollments. But these sensible reforms are being staunchly resisted by the teachers' unions and educational bureaucracy. Instead, additional billions are being proposed to perpetuate today's flawed system."

During the recent New Hampshire primaries, the *New York Times* pointed out in a profile of the Granite State that although New Hampshire is in the bottom ten states in spending on education, its students in the past 10 years have scored highest on the Scholastic Aptitude Tests (SAT).

The NEA would have a hernia explaining this one.

Bill Bennett, chairman of the National Endowment for the Humanities (NEH), was recently asked whether improving schools need cost billions of dollars.

"No," he replied. "All the literature we have on effective schools suggests that money is not the major issue. In fact much can be done to improve the schools at no cost at all."

Teachers are not primarily attracted to the profession because of money, Bennett said. "The best teachers are people who are dedicated to the education of the young, people who want to make a difference in the life of young people, a positive difference in molding their character and enhancing their minds."

This is illustrated by the fact that private school teachers, despite the fact that they make much less money than public school teachers, do a better job.

Most of the money the NEA wants is for itself, not for teachers anyway. The NEA wants to redouble its politicking efforts.

It is ironic, in view of this, that the NEA is a tax-free organization, exempt not by right (like churches) but by privilege, from paying taxes. The law says it is illegal for such groups to engage in partisan politics.

But in my view the NEA is breaking this law every week. The NEA admits its vigorous political involvements, indeed it admits its political priority.

While churches are being harassed, and their tax exemptions taken away because they do not dance to tunes played in Washington, the NEA is being allowed to go scot free. This is a very unfortunate situation.

Not only does the NEA back political causes, but it places itself squarely behind political candidates. If this isn't partisan, what is?

In 1976 the NEA endorsed Jimmy Carter who had pledged in return to form a Department of Education (DOE) and place it in the hands of the NEA. Carter staffer Thomas Dillon was quoted saying that "Teachers were critical to our success in 1976."

Carter repaid the NEA by forming the DOE, a bureaucratic boondoggle described by syndicated columnist Richard Reeves as "the largest political payoff in history."

Even Carter's top officials opposed the DOE. Joseph Califano, former HEW secretary, said, "We have a government plagued by special interests and the problem will be aggravated here because the special interest isn't even the group to be served—the children—but the NEA."

Not only did Carter ignore this advice and make the payoff, but he also persuaded Congress to increase federal spending on education by 73 percent from 1977 to 1980.

In return the NEA backed Carter to the hilt, even during crisis points in his presidency. For example the NEA opposed an investigation into Billy Carter's dealings with the Libyan government even though many Democrats called for this in the name of integrity.

Although the NEA denied that it was in cahoots with the Carter White House—a union which was an extended arm of the government—there are numerous documented connections which belie that claim.

Former NEA president John Ryor, for instance, played an important role on the Carter White House staff. Les Francis, former NEA organizer, was executive director of the Democratic National Committee. Fred Droz, former NEA official, was chief advance man for the Carter campaign. And William Mondale, the former vice president Walter Mondale's brother, was a top political strategist in NEA headquarters.

At the 1980 Democratic Convention the NEA was the most powerful power bloc. Earlier it had contributed, according to Common Cause a total of $420,787 to 147 out of the 210 Congressmen who had voted for the Department of Education.

Of the 3,331 delegates to the Democratic convention,

302 were NEA members. Of the approximately 2,000 alternates, 162 were NEA members. As one newspaper put it, "With almost 20 percent of the delegates needed to secure the Democratic nomination, the NEA is exercising a bigger role than any group in recent history."

Not only did the NEA attack candidate Ronald Reagan for opposing the Department of Education as a bureaucratic waste, but it also took its chance to attack an upcoming NBC film which it said featured "inappropriate racist, sexist, and violent material." The NEA also gave a "positive recommendation" for people to boycott the products of Nestle Corporation because it sold infant formula in Third World countries where misuse of the baby food has led to death and disease.

The NEA worked long and hard for Carter in 1980. It spent millions of its members money sending out mailings comparing the positions of Carter and Reagan on the issues. It reproduced Carter posters and gave them to schools. It made its computerized list available for pro-Carter propaganda.

Despite this Manichean campaign which depicted Ronald Reagan as the devil who opposed education and little children, and Jimmy Carter as the latter-day Messiah of education, the NEA was unable to convert its huge bankroll and sophisticated political machine into an electoral victory for its golden boy Jimmy.

Indeed it is estimated that 50 percent of the NEA's own members voted for Ronald Reagan.

What an insult to the NEA. What a waste of its members' money.

Unfortunately the Reagan administration has dragged its feet in getting rid of the DOE, despite the tremendous cost that this wasteful department imposes on the taxpayer.

Indeed Terrel Bell, whom Reagan named as Education Secretary, has become a strong advocate of keeping the department, to the chagrin of conservatives. Simply, Bell has sold out his boss Reagan.

Before the Reagan victory, NEA executive director Herndon said it might be "easier to let the education department go than to live with it under Reagan."

Unfortunately the NEA has not found the current administration very difficult to live with. The problem is not so much Reagan, who is well meaning but has other problems to deal with, but Terrel Bell.

When Reagan was first elected his chief counselor Ed Meese called the DOE "a ridiculous bureaucratic joke" and urged its dismantling. But why then did Reagan pick for this job Terrel Bell, who in the Carter years had actually testified before a congressional committee *in favor* of creating the DOE?

Bell fought efforts to severely cut the DOE budget. He asked Congress for a $13.5 billion budget for fiscal 1981, only 2.1 billion less than the Carter administration advocated. Congress gave Bell $14.8 billion.

Bell has either fired conservatives in the Reagan administration who continued to press for elimination of the DOE, or he has frustrated them into resigning.

For example Jim Lombard, a successful Florida businessman who gave up a six figure income to help undo the DOE, recently left the administration, citing frustration with Bell. "I was completely frustrated and realized I was not getting anywhere," he told *Reason* magazine.

So also Edward Curran, director of the National Institute for Education, wrote President Reagan urging the immediate abolition of his grants making agency which he called "wasteful and unnecessary."

However Curran's letter was intercepted by Richard Darman, top aide to White House Chief of Staff James Baker. Darman, who had helped *create* the National Institute for Education under President Nixon, contacted Bell, who had Curran fired.

Meanwhile Bell is hitting it off pretty well with the NEA and leftists in Congress. He tells union leaders, "I've been raising my voice for a moderate position with respect to the budget and with respect to the federal role . . . I haven't been for abolishing the federal role, as many feel to abolish the department means."

No wonder left-wing Democrat Paul Simon, Congressman from Illinois, says, "Anybody concerned about education should be grateful Ted Bell is down there."

Bell has not even been alert to gross violations of DOE grant rules. Last year the DOE's office of the Inspector General completed nine audits of Jesse Jackson's Operation PUSH, and concluded that of the $4.9 million given to the group from 1977 to 1981, nearly $2 million was spent in ways which violated federal regulations prohibiting political activity.

Why doesn't Reagan put Bell under the noose? Parents and those concerned with public education should push for this. Bell should get the same treatment as the DOE and the NEA: all three should be sent to the cleaners.

Because all three want more money for education but are either ignorant of the real problems facing education, or they are so concerned in furthering their own power and prestige that they don't care about these problems.

Despite the errors of his first term, Ronald Reagan remains a man of sound instinct as far as education is concerned. He is skeptical of the "experts" on this issue, and trusts communities and parents to run their own lives and to guide those of their children.

In other words, President Reagan is one of us, but Terrel Bell is not. Perhaps President Reagan does not realize this; it is one of the discoveries he is going to have to make, and we should help him make it.

The NEA is mounting pressure on Reagan. It has succeeded in gaining a $13.2 billion 1984 budget for the DOE. It has called for the federal government to provide one-third of all education spending (instead of the present 5-6%) which means the Treasury would have to increase the amount it spends currently on education six fold.

Imagine what that means in terms of the deficit. Imagine what that means in terms of taxes you are going to have to pay.

There is one way to avoid this potential disaster. That is to put pressure on the President to give Bell the boot and to put a genuinely pro-education (and pro-parent) person at the educational helm.

The NEA has already developed a "target list" of Congressmen it wants to defeat in 1984. Every single one is a Republican. Joe Standa, an NEA official, says these men have "anti-education" records.

The NEA also wants to defeat its number one enemy, Ronald Reagan.

Conclusion

Jacques Barzun is right when he says, in his classic book *Teacher in America,* "The once-proud and efficient public school system of the United States, especially its unique free high school for all, has turned into a waste land where violence and vice share the time of ignorance and idleness."

Largely responsible for this is the NEA, an organization which was formed for benign professional purposes, but has turned into a militant and savagely leftist union.

Why? As Mary Futrell, current president of the NEA explains, "When we were nice and polite, we didn't get anywhere. There's no alternative to political action. Instruction and professional development have been on the back burner for us, compared to political action."

Stunning. Futrell admits that the NEA is more concerned about politics than about either education, or the welfare of its members.

Once this was not so. The NEA was devoted to educational opportunity, not egalitarianism and world totalitarianism. The NEA was respectful of the economic freedom and the security of U.S. defenses which made its existence and freedom possible.

But now the NEA has gone from equality of opportunity to equality of result. It wants equality, which is equality of mediocrity or equality of ignorance, in the classroom: all intelligent students must be reduced to the level of the most disabled child. This prevents "elitism" in education.

The NEA also wants equality in the marketplace, which goes by the name of socialism. Goodbye, private property. Not only the US should be socialist, but the entire world:

indeed the NEA favors a world order presided over by some centralized bureaucracy, which would dictate rules from on high. Naturally the NEA wants to be part of that oppressive bureaucracy.

That an educational crisis presently exists in America cannot be doubted. But what is the NEA's response to this crisis, which it has helped create?

Columnist William Murchison puts it well: "First, to discredit the evidence of qualitative deterioration and the means of acquiring such evidence; second, to savage the critics of school equality; third, to mount elaborate campaigns to persuade the public that American education is basically fine, and that any minor problems would be solved by the application of more money; fourth, steadfastly refuse to let teachers be rewarded (or penalized) on the basis of their own, their pupils' or their schools' performance; fifth, to seek to control the agencies and the processes by which standards are set for students and teachers alike; and sixth, skillfully to employ the rhetoric of educational quality and excellence in advocating policies that would bring about nothing of the sort."

This catalog does not include the NEA's crusade for policies not connected in any way with education: nuclear freeze, U.S. nuclear disarmament, socialism, and world government. It is a measure of the NEA's insensitivity to the current crisis in education that it continues unhampered with its political agenda as if it had nothing better to do in the way of teaching and setting standards.

Fortunately, there is resistance building to the NEA's campaign to dominate and ruin public education. Most importantly, this campaign for centralization has been identified for what it is: an insidious power-grab.

Says Rep. John Ashbrook (R-Ohio), "An integral part of

the NEA design is to siphon off ever more control of public education from the grass roots to Washington, closer to its own powerful lobbying influence, farther from the parents and taxpayers who elect the school boards and pay the bills."

The issue has been clearly defined: the rights of the NEA, and special interest groups in general; versus the rights of parents, and democracy in general.

A number of organizations have been formed to fight for parents rights. One of the most prominent is the National Council for Better Education (NCBE).

An NCBE document states, "For 130 years the education establishment, embodied in the NEA, has dominated and controlled American education, promoting at each crucial juncture more state control and centralization to solidify their gains.

"But that liberal program has reached the end of the road. The disaster we face alone in growing functional illiteracy is enough to signal that a drastic change is needed.

"For us at the NCBE this is a momentous turning point—a great opportunity to seize the initiative and to restructure American education to reflect the wishes and values of the American people and not those of a small liberal elite.

"That is why we created the National Council for Better Education—an organization to harness the energy and vitality needed to create a new conservative educational agenda."

NCBE believes that each community should hire its own teachers setting its own criteria, choose its own textbooks, and structure its own curriculum. There is no need for a Washington bureaucracy to dictate and control our children's minds.

Parents should be free to transmit their religious and moral values to students. They should be able to use the schools for this if they wish. This is true freedom of religion, which the Constitution mandates; what groups like the NEA want is freedom *from* religion.

NCBE also intends to encourage private and home schooling so that parents have greater freedom to choose educational opportunities for their children. Also free competition between private and public education will improve both by forcing them to provide better education at lower cost.

NCBE stands in direct opposition to groups like the NEA, and to a lesser extent the AFT, which pretend to be in the interest of education, but which subvert their members interest and work to extend their own power.

Among the goals of the NCBE:

—To create a national communications program to inform the general public, the media, and lawmakers on the radical positions of the NEA.

—To promote and encourage local and community control of the public school. The NCBE does not have its own educational agenda. It supports the right of parents to set their own.

—To develop a network of intensive phonics instruction and make it available to those communities which want it. This is intended to reduce the shameful problem of illiteracy among our children.

—To establish a "teachers' division" concerned with the legitimate rights of teachers. This group will offer malpractice and health insurance and other consumer benefits.

—To design model programs for effective basic education, community-wide involvement, in-service instruction for teachers, and teacher training.

—To organize 50 state councils which will monitor the workings of the NEA and the Department of Education in each state, and fight for local and state control over education, resisting federal and centralized domination.

Perhaps the most ambitious program of the NCBE is its Educational Enterprise Zones (EEZ) concept. Here is how the NCBE explains it:

EDUCATIONAL ENTERPRISE ZONES

INTRODUCTION:

The Educational Enterprise Zone (EEZ) is a innovative, bold new concept developed by the National Council for Better Education (NCBE). It is intended to reduce centralized bureaucratic control of local schools, remove union restrictions and burdensome state regulations in a designated school district or zone, thereby promoting parental and community involvement. The prime objective of the EEZ is to return control of the school to the parents and community members.

We have all been inundated with a rash of educational reform reports in the last year, the most well-known being *A Nation At Risk* by the National Commission on Excellence in Education. The National Council for Better Education finds itself in complete agreement with the Commission's conclusions as to the problems that plague our public schools. It is in complete disagreement with some of their proposed solutions, however. For example, it is an insult to Americans of all ages to propose an increase in the federal role toward and the funding of schools, as the NCEE report does. Gallup polls show that Americans do not want extended school years or days. Parents believe that the quality of education is what is important—not the quantity. A recent *Conservative Digest* poll reported that 74% of the people polled believed that local school boards should have total control over what is taught. When will the bureaucrats in Washington listen to the voice of the citizens?

As federal and state funding has steadily increased over the past several decades, student achievement has steadily declined. There is wide agreement there are severe problems in todays schools. NCBE does not believe the solution is a continuation of the status quo.

The crucial solution in the '80's for these problems is educational reform. NCBE is convinced that parents must enter the debate. It believes our public schools cannot continue being the delivery system for social change. Schools must be reinstated as institutions to teach our youth the basic academic skills. Parents agree with these propositions.

PARENTS AND THE EEZ:

The most important aspect of the EEZ is its contention that the kind of instruction children receive is the responsibility of parents. The premise of the EEZ is that a school in a designated EEZ is an extension of the home. The training —social and academic—of a child thus is not the function of the federal government and only to a small degree that of the state. Herein lies one of the chief differences between a school in the public system and an Educational Enterprise Zone school. The public schools in the United States can properly be called "government schools" or "state schools" because they are owned and operated by the government. These schools start from the premise that the child while in school belongs to the state and is bound to serve the state.

An EEZ school, by contrast, is an extension of the home. Children in school belong not to the state, nor to themselves, but to the parents. The school and its staff should be an instrument of parents in carrying out part of their God-given responsibility. The parents and the school should enter into an arrangement to provide instruction whereby control remains in the hands of the parents. In the present system, parents are forced to support the school. The public school system thus enjoys a monopoly, and accordingly has very little incentive for improvement. The lack of accountability by teachers to parents adds to this lack of incentive. The principle of parental control over children has many implications in the areas of organization of the school: financing, discipline, curriculum, and so forth.

The model accepted by the National Council for Better Education's Educational Enterprise Zone is the private school. With less money and lower paid teachers, these schools consistently do a better job than public schools in educating children. James Coleman, a leading sociologist at the University of Chicago, has reported on over 60,000 high school students in public and private schools. Although this report provoked a lot of discussion and criticism, its most significant finding cannot be refuted: Both students and teachers in the private school work harder than their counterparts in the public school. Students are assigned more homework and teachers expect more of their students in the private school, and get more. The National Council for Better Education believes our nation's private schools have many valuable lessons to teach us and that is why we have modeled the basic tenets of the EEZ after them.

HOW TO ORGANIZE AN EEZ:

Many parents, in favor of a more involved parental role

in schools, have had difficulty translating this idea into reality from the public school's bureaucracy. The National Council for Better Education is convinced that many capable and well-meaning parents and other community members cannot use their influence efficiently towards reforming the public schools because of the organizational structure of the schools which they confront. The NCBE offers a plan for this purpose, the EEZ.

How will NCBE select the individual EEZ? We intend to go into a chosen school district and petition the parents and the citizens of the community, asking them if they would be interested in having their district designated as an EEZ.

When we find several that are open to the concept, and are able to get roughly 75% of the school district to sign a petition, the citizens can then go to the state legislature, introduce the EEZ legislation and proceed from there.

All parents and community members who wish to be included in the educational discussion effecting the EEZ, will be designated to man committees and subcommittees (along with teachers) appointed by the schoolboard.

The committees will be given the job, under guidance from the schoolboard, of developing a program that would address educational deficiencies in the designated area and provide solutions to these problems.

Example: 1) Curriculum development
2) Textbook selection
3) Teacher policies
4) Student policies

The chief characteristics of educational reform that committees should discuss are:

1) more order and discipline in the classroom
2) a halt to the use of classrooms for human potential experiments

3) a higher intellectual standard
4) adequate competency testing for students and teachers
5) more parental involvement in every aspect of education
6) less federal/state involvement in every aspect of education

Meeting approximately two to three times a month, on an ad hoc basis, the committee and subcommittees will look over several of the national and regional reports as well as several model programs appropriate to their committee's area.

Several matters will be affected by the type of organization in a particular EEZ, and most likely, no two EEZ's will be alike. Parents in Valley View, Texas might have quite a different perception of what they want their school to teach and what policies they wish it to implement, than parents in Idaho Falls, Idaho. Among the matters that will be effected: control of the school, curriculum selection, discipline codes, policies for teacher and student accountability, which includes hiring and firing policies.

After discussions, reviews and compromises are complete, the final draft of their proposed solution will be submitted to the school board for their review and (hopeful) implementation.

CONTENDING WITH GOVERNMENT REGULATIONS:

A major obstacle of parental control in public schools has traditionally been contending with cumbersome state regulations which effect the operations of the school in a variety of ways. EEZ schools will be free from binding regulations in the areas stated before.

A major study will be produced to enable us to determine which provisions of a given state education code and laws must be amended or "lifted" for a designated time period to permit parents and a community control of vital areas of their schools. The study will examine curriculum development, textbook selection processes, teacher hiring and firing policies, discipline and so forth.

Legislation will be drafted for the state legislature which will enable the schools to be liberated (for a designated experimental time period of 3-5 years) from unwarranted intrusions in these areas. Such legislation will allow the community to set up their own structure for decision making on these vital subjects.

We anticipate an inevitable conflict with state branches of the National Education Association (NEA). If defeated on a state level, the citizens can then use the initiative process and have it placed on ballots for voter decision.

CREDENTIALISM:

Parents and school boards if they so desire should be able to hire as teachers, able and enthusiastic people who don't necessarily have teaching certificates. A zone might wish to require that all of its teachers have a bachelors degree in the subject they wish to teach—maybe not. It may wish to provide competency testing before, during and after the teacher's tenure with the district. A zone may decide it wants new teachers to be intensively supervised by a senior (or mentor) teacher for the first year. Beyond that, performance should determine employment.

TENURE LAWS:

Most teachers receive tenure after three short years. This tends to protect many bad teachers by insuring their jobs indefinitely. Parents in an EEZ might wish to continue this practice or they may prefer to offer contracts of increasing duration—one, three, and then, five years for example.

Parents and school boards may wish to abolish tenure altogether to allow their school more flexibility in upgrading their teaching staffs. They may encourage people to enter teaching for short stints—injecting some youthful energy into the profession.

TEACHER COMPENSATION:

An EEZ might wish to raise or lower its district's pay scale. Many of the smaller, rural school districts do not have the available funds to pay their teachers above the state base. Even those districts that do might need to rearrange the pay scales on their teacher salary schedules. Some may wish to continue a practice of compensating teachers solely on the basis of seniority and college degrees. Others may wish to implement systems whereby teachers will be paid according to their performances, as measured by administrators, tests, fellow teachers, parents and students.

If a school in an EEZ wishes to pay what is necessary to attract quality teachers with the badly-needed skills in math and science, for example, they would be able to do so.

Several model merit pay plans, mentor teacher plans and evaluation systems will be made available to the EEZ in the form of an Educational Enterprise Zone Handbook (made available by a coalition effort on behalf of several major conservative groups). Parents and schoolboards may wish to choose one of these models or design their own, using various aspects of several model programs. Others may wish to implement their own ideas and suggestions.

DISCIPLINE:

We are not suggesting that a school, just because it has been designated as an EEZ, will be free of all discipline problems. Some children can never be transformed into attentive students, no matter how good are their teachers or the quality of their school environment. We do believe, however, that teachers must be given far more authority to rid themselves of troublesome students so they can pour their energies into teaching willing students. Once again, the best model for this purpose, is the private school.

TEACHER ACCOUNTABILITY:

The National Council for Better Education believes educators must be held accountable for their performance or lack thereof. Administrators must be given the power to make the necessary judgements about the abilities of our teachers. Without this, our schools are doomed to a future of mediocrity and failure.

The power of teacher unions must be broken in this area. Unpalatable as firing someone might be, sometimes it is necessary. That can be done best by administrators and without burdensome state laws and regulations tieing their hands.

CONCLUSION:

The point behind the ambitious EEZ plan is simply to return a significant portion of control and influence of education to the private sector. The National Council for Better Education does not intend to substitute its mandates for those of the state governments. We simply wish to provide the environment for parental involvement and the necessary materials that parent activists would need to make more responsible decisions about policies effecting their EEZ, their community, and most importantly, their children.

There is hope for American education. But constructive proposals like the EEZ must be pursued—and now. The problem is urgent: of that we must be alert. But the remedies also exist: of that we can be thankful.

Let us immediately set to work ridding ourself of the current educational establishment so that we can return control of education to parents, and stem the tide of mediocrity and illiteracy that is plaguing our public education system.

[ ] Enclosed is my check in the amount of $15.00 for membership in the National Council for Better Education. Make checks payable to:

National Council for Better Education.

_____

NAME

_____

ADDRESS

_____

CITY   STATE   ZIP

If you would like additional information on the *National Council for Better Education* please fill in the request below and send to:

National Council for Better Education
P.O. Box 37084
Washington, D.C.   20013

Please send information about the *National Council for Better Education*

_____

NAME

_____

ADDRESS

_____

CITY   STATE   ZIP

If you would like additional copies of **NEA: PROPAGANDA FRONT OF THE RADICAL LEFT,** please use the order blank below and send it along with your check to:

National Council for Better Education
P.O. Box 37084
Washington, D.C.   20013

1— 50 copies	$2.95 each
50—100 copies	1.95 each
100—500 copies	1.45 each
500 + copies	.99 each

Enclosed is my check for _____ copies of **NEA: PROPAGANDA FRONT OF THE RADICAL LEFT.**

Please send to:

_____
NAME

_____
ADDRESS

_____
CITY   STATE   ZIP

_____
PHONE #

Please make checks payable to:
        National Council for Better Education